How To Defuse The Landmines We Plant In Our Lives

By Kelly Accetta

Published by:

Westcom Press, LLC
10736 Jefferson Boulevard
Suite 383
Culver City, CA 90230

westcomassociates@mac.com

ISBN 978-1-938620-25-6

DEDICATION

Alexandra and Nicole, I dedicate my book to you, my amazing daughters. Thank you for all the patience and love you gave me as you grew up, while I was busy defusing my many landmines. My biggest blessing from God is being your mom.

CONTENTS

FOREWORD

There are people in life that you immediately connect with because you can see the soul and heart. Kelly is one of the best coaches I've ever seen.

All you have to do is look at the amazing family that she's raised and her ability through love, kindness and faith to communicate to every different level of society.

Her book and experiences will move you to laugh, cry, and make you introspective of your daily life. She is one of the coolest gatekeepers I've ever seen.

Nancy Lieberman,
Naismith Basketball Hall of Famer

INTRODUCTION

A strange encounter with a blind woman who could see better than most people with two good eyes inspired me to write *How to Defuse the Landmines We Plant in Our Lives.* I met the late Gail McWilliams at a women's conference, and we had a short but life-changing conversation.

Gail was a nationally known inspirational speaker, author, and radio-television host, and she described herself as "a visionary who inspires action." She'd just delivered an amazing inspirational message, and she was out in the church lobby selling her books and meeting fans. Since I love learning what makes us tick and I'm a voracious student, I bought her latest book. When I turned around, Gail was sitting right in my path, and at that exact moment, nobody was talking to her. I love the way God works!

I introduced myself and thanked her for sharing her thoughts. Before I could leave, Gail warmly asked what I did for a living. Now, that is a simple question with a complicated answer.

For the past twenty years, I've been a success coach. I

study what makes us women tick, how we process things the way we do, and why, oh why, we fall into the traps we set for ourselves. I travel around the globe, coaching, training, and speaking to amazing women of every type.

If only life were so simple! Depending on the hour of the day, I am also a bookkeeper, a property manager, a personal assistant, a financial forecaster, a marketing consultant, an accountability partner, a prop master, a costumer, a make-up artist, a logistics assistant, or a real estate investor. That's the long answer.

For the past ten years, my easy answer to Gail's question has been, "I'm a bookkeeper." That usually shuts down any further questions since most people know exactly what the job involves.

When Gail asked her question that day, though, I found myself blurting, "I'm a speaker/trainer."

As the words tumbled out of my mouth, I was embarrassed. You might think I was looking for common ground, or perhaps trying to impress her. Nothing could be further from the truth. I go out of my way not to divulge this to other speakers because I don't want to seem egotistical or appear like I'm one-upping them. (When someone does it to you, you realize how silly they sound.)

Of course, Gail's questions poured out: "Who do you train? How long have you been training? Do you have a special marketplace?"

Why *hadn't* I just said, "I'm a bookkeeper?" Well, I found out a few moments later when I summed up my life with one quick sentence:

"I train women how to defuse the landmines they've planted in their lives."

Gail looked straight at me (remember, she's blind), and she smiled. "Sounds like you have a great title for your next book!"

Until that moment, I'd never felt inspired to write a book, especially a personal growth and development book. Gail made me realize that my years of guiding women to be their best selves has given me something very valuable to share.

I hope you will gain insight and wisdom as I unfold the map of your personal minefield. I believe you can learn to see how destructive these landmines are to your life. Most important, I *know* you have the power to both defuse your own land mines and to stop planting them.

After you read this book, I encourage you to visit my website, *www.truth.coach*, for additional tools and support.

Best of all, I would love to spend some quality time with you at one of my workshops.

CHAPTER ONE

Landmine:
Insecurity

Oooooh—did I strike a nerve? "The landmines *you've* been planting?"

Yes, you read *that* right, and I'm proud of you for not getting pissy and tossing my book in the trash.

Let's get one thing straight: *You and I have never been wrong, neither have any of our girlfriends. In fact, it's a rare woman indeed that's ever wrong. I don't know if I've ever met one!*

Yes, I'm definitely being sarcastic. But I'm asking *right now*, *right* out of the blocks, for you to put your ego aside as you read this book. It's just you and me. I won't judge you, and you shouldn't either. Learning should never be a reason to beat yourself up even more than you already do.

Let's talk about the *real* reason why we women can't admit when we're wrong or make a mistake—*insecurity*.

How many times have you seen a woman sacrifice a friendship or a marriage because she *has* to be right?

One of my favorite expressions is, "Do you want to be right or happy?"

I know you're screaming at the book right now, "But what if I *am* right????"

So what if you *are*? Is it worth making the other person feel stupid and/or insignificant? No relationship can be successful without *mutual* respect.

> *Do you want to be right or happy?*

Unfortunately, we women are so insecure that sometimes we have to go around pointing out how wrong everyone else is. So, the next time you shut someone down and prove them wrong, ask yourself honestly if you did it out of unselfish love or because of your insecure ego.

Of course, we all need to be honest with the ones we love and tell them if they're in the wrong about things that really matter, but that's *not* what I'm talking about. I'm talking about the ego-driven, need-to-be-right, need-to-point-out-someone-else's-faults kind of honesty. Ego and pride will destroy *every* good relationship if they're not kept in check.

So how did we get this way? The Lord only knows!

We women have so many horror stories of how we ended up so insecure. Was it our parents, teachers, friends, abuse, the media, boyfriends? Who knows? It doesn't matter *how* we got there, how the landmine got planted in our minefield. It only matters that we defuse it.

Just like conquering any problem, recognizing that there *is* a problem is the first step.

I was horribly insecure and sometimes I still catch myself trying to replant that landmine. I know we all have different sources of our insecurity, but mine was triggered by male abandonment and betrayal.

My parents divorced and my dad left when I was eight. I found out he had been cheating on my mother with her best friend, a woman I considered to be my second mother. Like any young girl, I struggled with how my dad could leave me and how he could do such a horrible thing to my mom. Then my beloved older brother, who was my only rock at this point, moved to another state, and my other brother, deep in his own world of drugs, abandoned everyone.

I had another 12 years of other crap, even a rape, but it's not necessary to go into gory detail right now. I'm not telling you this to place blame or express bad feelings toward anyone in my family—they did what was right for them and they didn't do it to hurt me. I'm just telling you to explain that I had to figure out the source of my insecurity and deal with it. *I* had to forgive. *I* had to let go.

Ego and pride will destroy every good relationship if they're not kept in check.

Yes, I know how hard it is to forgive; I know you don't think I could possibly know, but I *know*! I also know that if you *don't* forgive, it's impossible to move on to a place where it doesn't hurt you anymore.

The people at the root of your insecurity don't sit around gloating about how they made you feel like a piece of chewed up gum on the sidewalk. They are probably so caught up in all of their own garbage, they haven't given it a second thought. Even if they are the evil sort and revel in the pain they caused you, *don't give them power to do so.*

Do you want them to win? Do you want to get to Heaven and see all the gifts and blessings God had in store for your life still sitting in a warehouse, waiting and unused, because you were too stubborn to forgive and could never move on and mature?

"But, Kelly, how can I forgive these persons for what they did to me?"

I hear you. I wish I had an easy answer. It might take some therapy; it might take confronting them. For *me*, it took God. I don't know what your answer will be, but now that you know forgiveness is the key to defusing the insecurity landmine, you can start working on it.

Stop letting this landmine blow up your confidence and relationships! Realize that you're the incredible person you are today because of what you had to endure. Which personality strengths and assets do you possess today *because* of the terrible things you went through? And lastly, no matter how bad you had it, realize some other woman suffered more than you did.

Before we go on, take a moment and write down the hurts you suffered and the personality assets they developed.

I'll start you off with a few of mine . . .

- Betrayal taught me to be loyal.
- Abandonment taught me to let the people I love know that I'm *always* here for them.
- Family alcoholism and drug abuse taught me there are no answers in coping that way, and to deal with emotional struggles in a positive way.

Now it's your turn:

_____(hurt)   taught me

_____

_____(asset)

_____(hurt)   taught me

_____

_____(asset)

_____(hurt)   taught me

_____

_____(asset)

_____(hurt) taught me

_____

_____(asset)

_____(hurt) taught me

_____

_____(asset)

_____(hurt) taught me

_____

_____(asset)

_____(hurt) taught me

_____

_____(asset)

_____(hurt) taught me

_____

_____(asset)

_____(hurt)   taught me

_____

_____(asset)

_____(hurt)   taught me

_____

_____(asset)

_____(hurt)   taught me

_____

_____(asset)

I hope that was revelatory for you. For some of you, there may be things that you suffered that are just too traumatic to see a positive outcome. Let me tell you, you have _tremendous_ strength inside you because you lived through it and survived. _That_ is your asset.

You might not have needed to tap into your strength yet, and you might not know it even exists. Believe me, sweet princess, the warrior within you will surprise you when the time comes to stand up for someone you care about (maybe even yourself).

Now, let's look at some of the shrapnel that can fly off this landmine when it's detonated: Self-promotion, jealousy, and fear are three of the most dangerous pieces of the insecurity landmine.

Self-promotion

Let's look at what my former co-worker Janet did to self-destruct. Janet got a job at the same company where I worked, and in the beginning, she was *amazing*. She ran circles around everyone in her department. She got there early, stayed late, helped anyone and everyone she could on whatever project they were working. I thought to myself, "Wow, I wish we had a few more of her around."

What I didn't know was the motivation behind her "work ethic," at least not until she had been with the company around six months and we went out to lunch.

We started out talking about the normal things but the conversation turned dark quickly. Janet told me that she works so hard because she wants to make it impossible for anyone to fire her. She has absorbed herself into so many projects and created ways to block anyone from accessing her work so that if they ever did fire her she could hold all these projects "hostage." She also laid out her strategy to get her boss fired by intentionally making him look incompetent.

I sat there as calmly as possible, but inside I was screaming, *What are you doing? You are on a path of self-destruction!*

I asked Janet, "Why do you feel all this is necessary? Why not just do a great job and honor those that have trusted you in that position?" She went on to explain that she had been fired from every job she had ever had and had never been with any one company longer than a year. (Ha, I wonder why?)

Since she wasn't in my department, I was torn about what to do. My young, inexperienced brain decided it wasn't my business to stick my nose in. I steered as clear of Janet as possible; that kind of toxicity never breeds anything positive.

It took another eight months for Janet's insecurity landmine to detonate and destroy her job, but what an eight months it was! Every meeting she was in, I watched nothing but her cutting people off mid-sentence, talking about how great she was, tearing others down publicly without ever speaking to them first privately about an issue, talking behind people's backs, spreading gossip, and so forth. I couldn't believe she hadn't been fired!

Well, one day the self-promoting monster Janet created through her insecurity came back to bite her.

The owner of the company stopped in to attend one of our all-staff trainings. He had been concerned over the company culture moving in a different direction, and he wanted to share his vision of where the company should go. As he turned to the white board to write something, he grabbed a sharpie rather a dry erase marker. In front of the entire company, Janet stood up and chastised him for being so careless. *Boom*, landmine detonated!

She was fired the next morning.

Self-promotion is probably the most annoying piece of the insecurity landmine, and unfortunately most people don't have the backbone to confront you if you do it.

Do you know anyone who practically breaks their own arm patting herself on the back? Someone who is constantly taking credit for things she has and hasn't done? Someone who hogs every ounce of spotlight and never shines the light on anyone else?

Make sure it's not you!

Insecurity creates a monster no one wants to be around on a regular basis. So how do you know if *you* are the monster? The best way is to be brave enough to ask someone who's around you most of the day. A trusted and mature co-worker; a spouse; a best friend. Make sure it's someone whom you trust who doesn't have some ulterior motive, like jealousy.

Most of us have a bit of insecurity and use self-promotion to some degree or another, but it's important to start catching yourself. At first, you'll catch it when you notice the reaction of the person you're talking to, then you'll catch it right after you say it, then you'll start catching yourself before you even utter a word. Success!

It just takes some awareness and practice. As your insecurities start to fade away, so will this annoying habit.

We have all felt the difference when we are confident in our job, our relationship, and the important parts of our lives, and when we're not. The problem is, when we are feeling insecure, we start looking around for someone else to blame.

Jealousy

Insecurity is 100% connected to jealousy—they go hand in hand. We hardly even need to discuss this one, it's so obvious. But we will anyway, it's too important and too destructive.

Jealousy can be all-consuming if we allow it to be. Unfortunately, in some cases, our jealousy will actually help bring about the awful consequences that we feared would happen. It's called the *Law of Attraction* and it's very real.

Though my friend Cheryl's boyfriend was super loyal and super in love with her, she was constantly jealous of any woman within five feet of him. She would accuse him of looking at the woman inappropriately. Other times, she'd throw out a line like, "You're late! Did you and (insert any female name here) have a good time?" Cheryl would sneak behind his back to try to find a text or an email to confirm her suspicions, and she confronted him on tiny, minor things.

After this went on constantly for a year with many different scenarios, Cheryl's boyfriend finally broke up with her. *Boom!* Now, could he have been unfaithful? It's always possible, but it really didn't matter. Her insecurities and fear caused her to be unfair and not trust him *before* he ever gave her a reason to not trust him. She drove him away.

We need to realize when we're the unhealthy one in the relationship.

If you are riddled with jealousy and fear, you truly are mentally abusing those closest to you. Now you're really screaming at the book, *But what if he **is** betraying me?* Well, then things will end anyway. But at least you didn't spend a year torturing him, your friends, and yourself.

When someone cheats on us, the root of our pain is usually our ego and pride. It hurts and we feel worthless, so our ego rears its ugly head. If we can take out the high drama and emotion and look at it for what it is, you'll see what just makes sense.

People don't cheat on someone they want to spend the rest of their lives with, so there is obviously a deeper issue with you, him, or even *both* of you that needs to be addressed and resolved. What you need to understand is that you weren't right for each other. It's *not* that there was something wrong with you.

Once the relationship ends, you'll need to be super

careful that you don't replant the insecurity landmine again. Realize he wasn't *The One* for you and be thankful that you are now free to go find *The One*.

Fear

When our insecurity is full of fear of failure, that's the most dangerous link. That fear can take us out, take us to our knees, cause us to sit down in our minefield paralyzed. The enemy would love nothing better than to see you give up on your dreams.

Failure is part of life, but it's also a huge part of success! Think back to when you were a kid and trying to learn something new—play a sport, get to the next level of a video game, get the boy you had a crush on to notice you, play an instrument, whatever. We endured failure after failure but kept going anyway if it was something we were excited about. We eventually got better until finally we were proficient.

I've heard it said that if we want to be good at something we need to invest about 10,000 hours doing it. How many of us as adults try to do something new just a few times, get discouraged, and give up?

You've known people who had a bad breakup and carried that baggage around *forever*, never allowing themselves to truly and deeply love again for fear of another rejection. You've also known people who were fired from a job, and they stopped trying to succeed and just hoped to hold on to whatever they could get.

Well, we can't score in a football game playing defense, and we certainly can't score in life either.

When I've dealt with a failure (and there have been *many*), I go back to focusing on my strengths, keeping my failure in perspective. (Is it *really* that big of a deal compared to all the horrible things going on in the world?) I also find it helpful at that time to serve others whose everyday challenges are so much greater than mine.

You're down, but you and I both know you won't be down forever, so why not just make the choice to get up now! Get to work creating your next opportunity to fail, learn, and succeed . Life is the great classroom, and we have to be willing to live and learn over and over and over so we can eventually graduate.

CHAPTER TWO

LANDMINE: VICTIM MENTALITY

We can start this chapter by looking back to Janet's story. At our one-and-only lunch, she never took ownership of even *one* of her firings. She told me about all five of them and it was never her fault. I'm sure after Janet was fired from our company, anyone she spoke to got an earful of how she was the victim in that whole situation. BOOM, another landmine detonated.

This landmine is personal and internal; very rarely does it affect anyone but the one with a victim mentality. How many years did Janet refuse to look in the mirror at her own actions that caused many of the negative outcomes in her life? I don't know. What I *do* know

Are you the victor or the victim in your life?

is that she will likely continue the cycle: Her insecurity landmine will blow up, and that explosion detonates her victim mentality landmine.

It's two for one.

"Why did she get the promotion?" "Why doesn't he give me more attention?" "Why does this always happen to me?"

Are you the *victor* or the *victim* in your life? Answer honestly. There's no growth without honest reflection.

If you're not sure if you're the victor or victim, here's an easy test to tell: Ask yourself if you have ultimate control over the events in your life that have a positive or negative impact on your emotional well-being. Do you find yourself blaming others for your situation at your job, the state of your happiness, the quality of your relationships? If you answered *yes*, I hate to break it to you—but you have another landmine to defuse.

Talk to any victor and they will tell you they and they *alone* control their ultimate happiness. It's not that bad things don't happen to them, it's how they *react* to those bad things that makes all the difference. Victims think they're always being singled out and picked on. Unfortunately, it goes right back to that first landmine we had to defuse, insecurity.

Victors in life are not those who get extra special treatment or skate through life; victors are those who can *truly* make lemonade out of lemons.

I want to share an amazing story of one of my all-time heroes, my grandfather, Art Arthur. When he was just a little boy in the Ukraine, violent anti-Semitic gangs were terrorizing Jewish people with massive massacres called pogroms.

The gangs descended on my grandfather's neighborhood and destroyed as many homes and beat to death as many Jews as they could. My grandfather's family hid, hoping and praying that they would somehow be spared. Their prayers were answered as the local police showed up when the gang was only two houses away.

Most of the neighborhood was destroyed and 50 to 100 neighbors died that day. Art's father, Zussman Bossin, gathered his seven children and all they could carry, and they left the home that had been in our family for generations. The family fled to Toronto, Canada, and had to start over.

Since my great-grandfather knew no English, his options were extremely limited in a big city, and he became a junk dealer. They lived in a slum called The Ward as he scoured the streets for scraps of junk to clean up and sell to make a living. He also helped to build one of the very first Jewish temples in Toronto and he learned English.

The living conditions in The Ward were horrific and cramped for the family that became ten. Even in these dire circumstances, Zussman made his children focus on their education. All went on to achieve great things, my grandfather in particular.

As a third grader, Art started working for the Toronto

newspaper as a newsboy, yelling EXTRA, EXTRA on the street corner. Within a short time, he had worked his way up to assistant for the famous Walter Winchell. When Walt went to New York City, he brought my grandfather with him.

Eventually Art got his own "beat" for the Brooklyn Daily Eagle and was cultivating a great career in the newspaper business. But Art wanted to do more, so he moved out to Hollywood to become a screen writer, worked his ass off like his father taught him, didn't let rejection slow him down, and he got his dream. My grandfather wrote close to 20 films that were released in theaters, wrote most of the *Sea Hunt* TV series, numerous episodes of *Daktari*, *Flipper* and *Gentle Ben*, was the Unit Supervisor for Cecil B. DeMille on *The Ten Commandments*, and much more.

Art's greatest professional achievement was a documentary. In his 40s, while Hitler was creating chaos in Europe, my grandfather answered the call. He was too old and he was a Canadian citizen, but he answered anyway. He applied and received his U.S. citizenship and left his wife and child to go fight the Nazis with a pen.

My grandfather was part of a team of writers responsible for much of the news that kept the world informed about the atrocities being carried out by the Nazis. At the end of the war, he stayed on to cover the crippling effect the war had had on Europe, especially its children. He wrote the hauntingly brilliant documentary, *Seeds of Destiny.*

The documentary was repeatedly shown in a Capitol Hill screening room and it became a major inspiration for Congress to pass the Marshall Plan of 1947. The Marshall Plan provided critical aid to Western Europe that helped combat hunger, poverty and disease. The documentary also won an Academy Award.

As great as those things are, they pale in comparison to what, in my opinion, was the greatest accomplishment of that movie. A British delegate to the UN, Philip Noel-Baker, saw *Seeds of Destiny* and he was profoundly moved. He quickly arranged for the entire UN delegation to see it by playing it every day before their meetings began.

It was in Geneva in 1946 that this little 21-minute documentary shaped United Nations policy and UNICEF was created. By 1955, UNICEF reported that over one hundred million children had been helped in only nine years. More than seventy years after it was founded, UNICEF is in 190 countries and is still saving millions of children's lives.

I told you this story to ask you this: What if my grandfather just sat on his hands and played the victim? He could have said so many times, "They stole everything from me;" "I don't have enough education;" "I'm an immigrant;" "I'm a Jew and suffer persecution from so many sides;" "How could I ever compete with the reporters in New York City?;" "How on Earth could I ever write a screenplay?;" "*Another* rejection notice;" "I'm too old to have any impact in such a big war;" or even, "I'm only one person, what can I do?"

All of those statements have *victim* written all over them. Thankfully, my grandfather was the ultimate *victor*. Nothing stood in his way, but more importantly, *he* didn't stand in his own way.

> *Your goal is to . . . go into problem-solving victor mode.*

That's the real obstacle for people with a victim mentality—themselves.

Come on, be honest. How many of us, when we're faced with a really big problem or dealt a really shitty hand, have thrown ourselves a big ass pity party—and then eventually, when we finally dealt with the problem head-on, we figured a way out of it.

When we allow ourselves to wallow around as a victim, we stop the thinking process and get tied down in emotion. Let's be real, most of us *don't* make great decisions when our emotions are out of control, riding on a rollercoaster.

Well, I have some great news. Defusing this landmine is very simple—not easy—*simple*. First, you have to catch yourself doing it. Being a victim has probably become a habit. Again, don't get defensive right now. The only way to improve is to be honest with yourself. If you have a hard time catching yourself doing it, empower your spouse/significant other/best friend to point out when you're doing it. (Believe me, they already do that in their mind.)

The key is to not get mad at them or defend yourself when they point it out to you. Pick out a code word (*pizza*, *Mt. Everest*, something) so that there's no need to have an emotional discussion about it, so you can start recognizing just how often you're being a victim.

Your goal is to jerk yourself out of the victim's stagnation swamp and go into problem-solving victor mode.

You want to hear that code word less and less every day, and then less and less every week. As you create a new habit of responding to smaller challenges in your life, you'll be a well-trained soldier for when the *real* battles show up.

Another effective tool to defuse the victim landmine is to volunteer somewhere to get a true perspective of your life. Go serve the homeless one of the few hot meals they might get all year, volunteer at a safe house for battered women, go to a third-world country where mothers have to choose which child to feed and which to let die of hunger because there's not enough food to keep both alive.

How bad do you *really* have it?

Even as I'm writing this right now, I'm going through one of the toughest times in my life emotionally. But it doesn't matter! Nothing and no one has permission to steal my joy. *I will be a victor!*

You will always have problems rear up in your life. Will you lie down and find someone to blame, or will you rise up and make those circumstances define a new challenge and an opportunity to see what you're made of?

You have a choice!

CHAPTER THREE

LANDMINE: GOSSIPING

Whew, we've tackled two very deep and confrontational landmines just now. Don't be surprised if you need to blow up these landmines a few more times before you become adept at not letting yourself slide into insecurity or a victim mentality. Just don't get down on yourself when you stumble. Get yourself back up, brush yourself off, and it will get easier and easier the more you work on defusing them.

So, let's talk about gossiping! Gossiping might seem like such a harmless landmine, one you don't even mind being there, but it's a *real* landmine and I guarantee it'll blow up at some point and destroy your relationships.

Why do we women love to gossip? It's such a common thing that we do, it's even written into most female roles in movies and television. Men do it too, but not near as often as women and usually without the consequences.

There are two huge problems with gossiping.

Gossiping replants your insecurity landmines. We

usually engage in gossip because we are jealous and insecure. Why do we look at another human being, one of God's children, and feel we have the right to judge them about *anything*?

> *There will always be gossips—just don't be one of them.*

A Bible verse that I constantly repeat to myself is, *"Judge not, lest you be judged."* It's easier to find fault with others so we don't have to face our own faults. It's wrong, it's destructive, and it feeds our insecurity. We've got to get out of the proverbial gutter and start taking the high road.

I know, I know, you're saying, "Kelly, I just need to vent about these people that are driving me crazy. They're so full of themselves, they're so annoying, they're such a slut, they have no taste, etc. etc., it's just a little harmless gossip, no big deal."

Let me ask you another tough question that asks you to be painfully honest with yourself again:

Have *you* ever made a mistake, said or did something you regretted? Have *you* worn an outfit that missed the mark, or had a really bad hair day?

Of course you have, we *all* have.

You probably didn't stop to realize there were snotty people talking about you behind your back. Now, I'm not saying that you should start caring about what people say behind your back. There will always be gossips—*just don't be one of them.* If you don't feel good about yourself unless you put others down, you will have a really hard time finding true happiness in life.

The other downside about gossiping is what I alluded to earlier. Men will gossip, too, but they're less likely to share what they heard. On the other hand, how many times have you had a girlfriend call you on the phone or pull you into a quiet place and say something like, "Oh my god, just *wait* 'til you hear what I just heard!" We love to gossip, we love to perpetuate gossip, we love to hear other's gossip; what on Earth is wrong with us?

Our gossip always gets back to the person we've been talking about. *KaBoom*! Landmine detonated! Now you have a big mess to try to clean up: Relationships are fractured, people take sides, feelings are hurt.

Who is this person you gossiped about? Your boss? Your best friend? A co-worker? Your spouse? You violated their trust by talking behind their back, and now you will pay the consequences.

Passed over for a raise or a promotion? Lost your best friend and most of the circle of friends you had in common? That co-worker is now spreading gossip about you all over the office? Your spouse is distant and disrespectful because of the hurt he feels?

Was gossiping *really* worth it? Is it *really* harmless? The answer is a resounding *NO!*

So how do you defuse this landmine? Easy. Just stop!

First, stop gossiping yourself. Learn to hear yourself as you talk about someone else. Are you being critical? Judgmental? Are you saying *anything* that you haven't already said or would be willing to say to their face?

Stop immediately! Apologize to the person you're talking to, and then drop it.

Right now, you might be thinking, "Why do I need to apologize to *her*? I wasn't talking about her." Your apology may actually keep her from sharing and perpetuating your hurtful words, and that could quite possibly prevent the words from getting back to the person you were gossiping about.

The most important reason might not be that obvious. Let me share one of my favorite quotes: "Don't treat people like they're stupid. The stupid people won't notice, but the smart ones will."

Whenever someone tries to share some gossip with me, I stop her as politely as I can, while I think to myself, "Wow, I wonder what she says about *me* when I'm not around."

After a gossip session, women who are unaware won't think twice about what others say behind their backs, but aware women will; they'll never trust you with their hearts. What kind of relationships can we build if we don't share our hearts with each other?

Stop listening to gossip. I told you that when people

come to me and want to gossip about someone, I won't listen. Instead, I defuse the gossiper's landmine. First, I'll try to change the subject. If that doesn't work, I'll try to defend whoever she's talking about by offering an insight or theory of why that person might have done or acted the way they did.

If that *still* doesn't work, I stop the gossiper in her tracks, and say, "Have you said all this to that person face-to-face? I don't feel it's healthy to discuss this behind their back. You should really try to take all of this to them directly."

Gossip is only fun when there's a willing listener, so don't be one.

I want to be clear about what gossip really is. There are times you must discuss issues that concern others. Gossip is not when someone asks you to help solve a problem between them and someone else with whom you have insight or influence.

To keep discussion out of the realm of gossip, I have a nonnegotiable rule: Whenever I'm speaking about a person who isn't right there with me, I pretend they've planted a listening device and have direct access to what's being said.

This rule keeps me from saying anything that I wouldn't say to someone directly. It also helps me with *how* I say it, the tone of my voice.

If an employee is rude to customers and the manager

brings it to my attention, I'm aware it's important that my tone never sounds like I condemn or don't respect the employee we're discussing. Though I'm hardly perfect, I know that I'm much better than I used to be, and I'm getting better every year.

It truly breaks my heart if something I say gets back to someone and hurts their feelings or self-esteem. This is why talking directly to the person involved is *so* important. You can take something that could hurt someone if they heard it indirectly and turn it into a great opportunity to mentor them.

More than twenty years ago, I trained a young sales rep in Dallas. Billy was a charismatic, good-looking, energetic kid who wanted to succeed at the highest level in our company. There was one minor problem—both his ears were pierced and he wore small hoop earrings.

Now remember, this was in the 1990s in conservative, Bible Belt Dallas. Billy looked very cool to his peers, but when he made sales presentations to older prospects, it was clear they didn't take him seriously. I didn't want to hurt his feelings, but I knew those earrings were the problem.

I didn't say anything for weeks, until one day when my mentor asked me how Billy was doing. After I explained what I thought the problem was, I proceeded to get chewed out for what seemed like forever! But my mentor had a great point. All of us in the office saw the talent in this kid, but we talked among ourselves about how detrimental those piercings were to his sales numbers instead of talking to *him*.

My mentor gave me the uncomfortable task of telling Billy, and *wow*, was it hard! Using the coaching I had received from my mentor, I tried to be as respectful as I could be.

"Billy, you are a really talented guy, and you work hard. We all think you deserve to succeed. Unfortunately, I think your earrings are probably costing you sales with our conservative clients. Although it isn't fair for people to judge us by our outward appearance, that's unfortunately what most humans do. Let's conduct an experiment. Take out your earrings for three months and let's see how your sales improve."

We need to start focusing on the things that unite us.

Well, talk about a home run! His sales went through the roof, which in turn helped his confidence and ultimately his income. Needless to say, after the three months were over, he didn't go back to wearing his earrings.

Billy went on to become a top producer for the company where we worked together for the next ten years, then he moved to another company where he's even more successful. After more than 20 years, we're still friends. I'm so thankful that I was pushed into turning office gossip into an opportunity for growth.

Stop buying gossip and don't watch it on TV or online.
This is the last step to dismantling the gossip landmine.
As a group, we women are responsible for the scourge
called paparazzi. It's so sad that famous people and
their families have no privacy, *ever*, even on a family
vacation, because we want to catch the pretty, popular,
successful, people with their gut hanging out or without
make up. How twisted is that?

Very few men read gossip magazines or watch
shows like TMZ. It's just us, the insecure little girls who
desperately want to feel better about ourselves. Gossip
brings us right back to having to defuse the insecurity
landmines that we planted—again.

As women, we need to stop focusing on the things
that divide us and start focusing on the things that unite
us: our nurturing spirits, our multi-faceted personalities,
our strength and resolve when we protect those that we
love, our ability to wear five different hats all in the
same day (if not the same hour).

Instead of getting pleasure from our sisters'
problems, maybe we need to look at these women
with understanding and realize they're probably going
through "stuff" too. Let's give them the same grace we'd
love for them to give us.

CHAPTER FOUR

LANDMINE: BACKSTABBING

You might ask, isn't backstabbing the same as gossiping? Not at all. Backstabbing, or being two-faced, deserves its own place in your minefield. Be aware, the guys plant this landmine, too.

I was born and raised in Southern California, and we Californians are known to be pretty phony as a whole. But, as much as I love most of the people in my hometown of the last twenty-plus years, Dallas takes the prize for backstabbing. Wow, was I shocked by how many women and men would say something publicly, but when they were in private, they were *completely* of a different opinion.

At a charity event, an acquaintance walked up to say hello to me and a casual friend we both shared. The so-called friend I was standing with went on and on about the other woman's new hairstyle and how much she loved it. As soon the woman walked away and was out of earshot, my friend told me how awful she thought the hairstyle really was. *BAM*, landmine detonated!

How could I ever trust another word out of my "friend's" mouth? Why didn't she just be quiet and say nothing?

Say what you're going to do and do what you say.

I love that the word "authentic" is now getting thrown around, like it's a new concept. How *else* has everyone been living? It's comical; even companies are bragging about their new corporate initiatives to be "transparent" and "authentic." I don't want to surround myself with people and companies that have to sell me on their authenticity.

It's easy—*say what you're going to do and do what you say*. A dear friend of mine has a life motto that his word is his bond, and he rarely signs contracts with business associates. When I asked him why, he said, "Because I don't do business with people who don't do what they say."

Granted, my friend is from a different time and generation than most of us, and I'm certainly not recommending that you don't sign contracts. Still, imagine how awesome it would be, surrounded by people without a two-faced bone in their body. What kind of relationships could you have with these people, how much trust could you have? Defusing this landmine is *very* important to your long-term happiness and there are two parts to defusing it.

First, you have to stop being a backstabber and two-faced yourself. (Have you noticed a common theme in my book?) There is no faster way to lose people's trust than to say one thing and do another.

Sometimes, you're intentionally being two-faced; you don't want someone to know how you really feel about something. In that case, say *nothing*! Yes, I said, "Say nothing." Wow, this is hard for women. We have an opinion about *everything* and it's a knee-jerk response to say *something* so we tell "little white lies." A *lie* is a *lie*, and if you get caught in that lie (white, black, or purple), you will violate trust.

My true friends tell me the truth; I don't always like it, and I don't always agree, but I know they have been honest. Some of you end friendships when someone says something you don't like; to *me*, that person is someone I want in my life forever.

Other times, it's unintentional. How many times have we told our kids, spouse, client, or friend that we would do something, and then we didn't do it. We women tend to overcommit our schedules; I have been so guilty of this over the years. Thankfully, honest people in my life pointed out to me that over commitment is a lie. Ouch! It's unintentional, but it still has the same consequences—it's two-faced. If you say one thing and do another often enough, the people in your life will stop trusting you.

Second, remove two-faced people from your life. Don't you deserve honest, truthful, "authentic" friends? People who don't let you down? Yes! But remember, you can't ask that of others if you don't hold yourself to the same standard, so you can't start on this part until you fix *you*.

Once that is done, you can start having conversations with your close circle of family and friends and tell them about your change of heart. Take these steps in order.

- Explain that you want to start building true, trusting, deep relationships.
- Tell them you want them to be completely honest with you *if you ask them* for their opinion on any matter, even if they think you disagree with them.
- Let them know you value their input even if you don't go in the direction they recommend.
- Ask if you have permission to do the same when they *ask*. The "asking" is obviously critical. No one wants to get a running commentary on how they should be living their lives all day.
- Don't be defensive.

Defensive behavior is actually a whole other landmine that we can just address in a few sentences; it doesn't need a whole chapter.

Here is the bottom line: If someone takes the time to give us input in a sincere and loving way, we can't bite their heads off for what they said. If we do react negatively or defensively, they'll just go back to lying to us.

You need to make sure input and reaction are done in a sincere and loving way, in both directions. There can be damaging consequences if either party laces their comments with sarcasm or reveals privately discussed matters in public to intentionally cause embarrassment.

We can't learn if we talk and never listen.

Defensiveness blocks the process as thoroughly as sarcasm or indiscretion, however. Every mature adult who has ever tried to mentor someone can attest to the frustration that defensiveness causes. If someone corrects us or asks a simple question in a respectful way, and we respond defensively, we may have a deeper issue.

I did this unknowingly for *years!*

Anytime someone corrected me or gave me constructive input, my insecurity landmine blew up and I became defensive. I'd start in with my excuses because I didn't want anyone to think of me as incompetent, stupid, ignorant, weak, worthless . . . sound familiar?

These people saw *value* in me! That's why they wanted to help me do better. They liked and respected me! That's why they poured their valuable time into me.

We can't learn if we talk and never listen. There's actually a great quote from the Dalai Lama: "When you talk, you are only repeating what you already know. But if you listen, you may learn something new."

Now I go out of my way to never be the smartest person in the room. By this, I mean I want to surround myself with more successful people in all areas of life, then listen and learn.

As you make these wiser and more successful friends and mentors, keep this new perspective in the front of your mind: *You'll never gain the benefit of their wisdom if you become defensive when you hear information different from what you currently believe.*

CHAPTER FIVE

LANDMINE: OFFENDABLE

I know it might be hard to believe, but a batch of women have already stopped reading this book because they were offended by something in my first four chapters. Maybe they closed the book because I used an off-color word, maybe because I said something that struck a nerve, or maybe because I wrote the word "God."

The reason doesn't really matter; these women cut off the learning process because it didn't fit within their belief systems.

Congratulations to all of you that are still with me! Being offendable or easily offended is a nasty landmine, and if it's not defused, it will stifle learning and growth throughout your *entire* life.

I'm reminded of Barbara, a woman that I met almost twenty years ago at a wonderful two-day seminar. It was given by a prominent, successful entrepreneur in our field, and the seminar ran from 8 a.m. to 6 p.m.

on Saturday and Sunday. If you subtract the hour we took for lunch each day, we received a full 18 hours of valuable information from this expert.

About two-and-a-half hours into the seminar, we had a quick break between sessions, and Barbara and I headed out of the ballroom together.

I asked her, "Do you want to grab a coffee before the next session?"

Why do we give so much power to words?

"*I* won't be returning." She sounded a bit frosty.

I was shocked. "I'm sorry! Are you feeling all right? Do you have a family emergency?"

Barbara turned to me with a smug look. "I was so offended, I'm won't step a foot back into that room. The speaker referred to women as *girls!*"

BOOM!!! She blew up a perfectly good opportunity because she allowed herself to be offended. (The speaker only said "girl" once, by the way.) The funny thing is that he didn't even notice she didn't come back. Wow, she showed *him!*

What really blew my mind was that she heard *nothing* of the incredible things he taught in that session, only the word "girls." Not to mention the full two days of business-changing, out-of-the-box and out-of-this-world information that unfolded during the remainder of the seminar.

That weekend was a true game changer for my career. I implemented most of what the seminar taught and saw my business and my income explode.

As for Barbara: Six months later, I ran into someone who worked with her, and asked how she was doing. Barbara had quit.

How many opportunities for growth and learning have *you* blown up because you were "offended?" How many relationships?

Here is the most important question: Why do we give so much power to *words*? As a society, we are in a constant state of craziness trying to keep our words inoffensive and "politically correct." It's *exasperating* to try to keep up!

I was blessed to have had the privilege of taking care of my special-needs brother-in-law for almost ten years. One time when I was trying to find a social program for him, I asked a woman on the phone if her son was "special," and she about hung up on me. It seemed the word "special" without the "needs" was now insulting.

You and any other human who become offended by just a *word* are ridiculous! (Oops, did I offend you?) It's not the *word* that you should be concerned about, it's the *emotion* behind it!

The man leading the seminar didn't use a derogatory tone when he said "girls," and the funny thing is he also referred to men as "boys" in the same sentence. We have to use common sense (which, by the way, is not very common out there in the real world). Our brains should pick up the tones and nuances like sarcasm, hatred, bigotry, and, most importantly, *ignorance.*

When I say ignorance, I don't mean stupidity. Ignorance just means you don't know something. I am ignorant of so much in this world, and if I do or say something out of ignorance, I would hope someone doesn't bite my head off and accuse me of being stupid or insensitive. I would hope that they use their common sense to give me the benefit of the doubt and realize it was an honest, ignorant mistake made by someone with a good heart.

A perfect example is football. I'm not a big fan, but I watch it here and there, and I've accidentally used the wrong football term out of ignorance. What kind of a jerk would become offended and scold me for being so "stupid?" Wouldn't you want someone to politely and privately educate you on the proper term? *Of course!*

It's not just words that offend us ladies, unfortunately actions seem to offend us as well. Maybe these phrases sound familiar:

"I can't believe he did that to me!"

"I can't believe *she* got the promotion!"

A friend recently called me from her job, complaining about how a new hire was dressing. I asked, "Why are you so offended? Maybe she doesn't have anyone to teach her, maybe instead of being so offended you should step in and be her mentor! *I* was this girl 28 years ago!"

Yes, it's true. I was working in a professional office right out of college, and my wardrobe consisted of jeans, shorts, t-shirts, sweatshirts, and clubbing outfits, all typical of any college female in San Diego. So, I came to work in my "club" clothes because they were the dressiest clothes I owned and I thought they were cute. Thankfully, a woman just a few years older than me took me under her wing. She mentioned that she was cleaning out her closet over the weekend and wanted to know if I would like to stop by and take anything she was getting rid of.

Of course, being a broke twenty-something, I jumped at the chance of free clothes. While I was at her apartment, she took the opportunity to teach me a few things about proper office attire in such a sweet and funny way. I loved her for that, I respected her for that, and when the time came down the road I paid it forward and helped many young, up-and-coming women with clothes and guidance.

The offendable landmine is so easy to defuse; let me explain how. Most of the other landmines are harder to detect because they've become habitual actions or responses, ones we don't even realize we're engaging in. Being easily offended, on the other hand, is obvious because it elicits such a strong, immediate reaction.

When we're offended, all we need to do is breathe

and evaluate. Breathing is key to preserving your joy, which you should *never* allow someone to take. Evaluating is key to how you respond.

> *You should know who you are, but more importantly, you need to know whose *you* are.*

Was it a misstep out of ignorance? If it was, privately take a moment to let the offender know how it might be interpreted by others, and that you wouldn't want people to misunderstand their heart. You can do this by email or text if you can't get a moment alone with them.

I've done this hundreds of times and people are always grateful.

Was it a misstep out of hatred, prejudice, or stupidity? Unfortunately, that will be the case sometimes. I was in Alabama at a grocery store just six months ago when the man behind me in line made a derogatory and racist comment about the cashier. I was offended for her, I was hurt for her. Thankfully she didn't hear what he said, but I couldn't just be quiet. When she turned her back to get change from another cashier, I said my piece:

"*Wow*, I didn't know racists still existed. The rest of the world has actually picked up a book or two and realized the only difference between a human being preciously created by God is what's on the outside. We are *all* different on the outside but the same inside. Should I mock or judge you because you have brown eyes and I have blue? No, that would be stupid. We all bleed the same, our hearts beat the same, we all want to be loved, we all want the best for our families. I hope you ask God to soften your heart and ask to see His precious children through His eyes."

Now, could this man have just walked away? Yep. Should I care? Nope. Forest Gump said it best, "stupid is as stupid does." Why let some jerk ruin your day, week , or year?

Stop being offendable, let it go, it's their problem, not yours. You should know who you are, but more importantly, you need to know *whose* you are. You are beautifully and wonderfully made by your Awesome Creator, the same Creator that made the oceans, the mountains, the sunsets. He created everything perfectly; even imperfection is perfectly imperfect.

By social standards, my brother in-law was imperfect, but for those of us willing to look closer, we got to see God's perfection in him. There was nothing about him that ever offended me.

By the way, the man in Alabama felt very badly about what he had said, and he apologized. Who knows if he was sincere. If he was, though, hopefully he'll look closer and start seeing the beauty in all the differences and imperfections of people.

CHAPTER SIX

LANDMINE: MOMMY GUILT

(Do not skip this if you're not a "mom")

I t was picture day. *I forgot.*

Those of you without kids might not see why that's such a big deal. Let me explain. My girls were six and nine, and they needed my help with their long hair every day. On this particular morning I was "teaching" them to be responsible and get themselves ready for school.

When they finally ran downstairs, it was clear that they'd gone back to sleep after I woke them an hour earlier. They were wearing disheveled, stained school uniforms, obviously grabbed from wherever they'd dropped them the day before, and their hair was a tangled mess. We didn't have time to change or brush their hair, and I figured they would learn a valuable lesson, so we just left for school.

As I walked through the door at their school and saw all the little girls with perfectly coiffed hair, decorated with ribbons and sparkles, and the boys wearing their neat little ties, it hit me like a ton of bricks! I quickly grabbed a brush from my purse and tried desperately to brush their hair but I was just making it worse. When my girls realized it was picture day, the tears began slowly rolling down their sweet little cheeks—*BAM!*

Almost all women will have children in their lives—and I'm not counting just the ones women bear themselves. Their children may be borne by another woman, they may be furry, and sometimes it's a classroom full, or even a country. Being a mother is about having a deep love and need to protect and nurture. Mother Theresa didn't give birth to a single child, but she had tens of thousands of children. I say all this to explain that this deep love also comes with its own big landmine: *guilt.*

How sad that we use one of our strongest assets for our own destruction. I can't begin to tell you how many thousands of women I've coached over the last 20 years who have beaten themselves bloody because of mommy guilt. Let's not stop there: Often it's just plain guilt.

Women come to me in tears, crying, "I just can't be everything I should be to my kids, my husband, my job, my house, my church," and on and on. I often hear, "I feel like I'm letting *everyone* down;" "I feel like I'm not doing anything right."

Do you relate? Are other people you love also stuck

in this horrible cycle? Then read on and learn how to defuse this torturous landmine.

First, let's take a second to breathe. For some of you, I just sprinkled salt into a gaping wound. You are not alone in this struggle, it's *the* most common landmine I have found in women across all races, cultures, and countries.

I have spoken on mommy guilt in North America, Europe, Africa, Asia, and Australia, and my words have been translated into 25-plus different languages. I always have a crowd of women weeping tears of joy when I've helped them defuse this one.

Eleanor Roosevelt said it best, "No one can make you feel inferior without *your* consent." Again, this starts with us. I am speaking from first-hand experience because I lived through defusing this one over and over and over; guilt was the toughest for me to eradicate from my minefield.

Let's get to work on ridding your minefield of this once and for all.

Unfortunately, the media and society (especially social media) have put an immense amount of pressure on us moms. Let's just pause and look at a little history of mothering and get some perspective.

It wasn't long ago that a woman had her baby, wrapped it in a sling, carried the baby on her body, and went about doing what she needed to get done. When that child could walk, he or she joined in the work of the day. We moved from that to our grandparent's generation, when most parents told their kids to speak when spoken to, and above all, respect your elders. Mothers shooed their kids out of the house as soon as chores were finished so they could get their housework done.

Let's think about that: Mothers had to make three meals a day from *scratch*, wash and dry the dishes by hand, clean the house without things like paper towels, effective solvents, or vacuum cleaners. And laundry! Most families had many more kids than they have today, and our grandmothers had to wash it all by hand (maybe they had a washing machine), then hang every piece on a line to dry, fold it, and divvy it out to everyone in the house.

Even my mother's generation was pretty hands-off. I remember getting up for school, making my breakfast, packing my lunch, and heading out to school with a kiss on the cheek and a "Have a great day." When I got home, I quickly did my homework, then headed outside to play and didn't return home until the streetlights came on.

When I came in dinner was almost ready (rarely made from scratch), and we all sat down at the table and caught each other up on our days. After dinner, a shower, maybe a little TV snuggled up on the couch, and then bedtime. Never did I feel ignored or unloved.

How in the world have we gone from that relaxed parenting to this kid-centric craziness that's taken over our lives today?

From the minute we have a baby nowadays, we are expected to be super moms that do anything and everything for that child's happiness

Let it go and let them grow

and security. Is it working? Is this really a better way?

I don't know for sure, but I do know I learned a lot about how to be self-sufficient, confident, how to solve disputes, how to communicate my emotions, and how to win from everyone else *other* than my mom. Don't get me wrong, my mom was very loving and encouraging, but most kids know their mom thinks they're awesome.

It takes a lot of little failures in friendships, team sports, competitions, school, paper routes, even babysitting, to learn how to do things right. When adults other than our mom gives us a compliment or a correction, their words carry so much more weight.

Don't even get me started on the whole "everyone gets a trophy" crap. That trend has helped to produce the most entitled batch of young adults that know very little about what it takes to actually win in life. Their precious little hearts were protected from finding out that they didn't work hard enough, practice when they should have, condition harder, or seek out an expert for help. Now guess where they get to figure this all out—the *real* world, when their job or a crucial relationship is on the line. So, **stop! Stop** running around in a frenzy trying to be super mom.

The very first thing you need to do is take inventory of what you are doing for your kids, then ask yourself, "Can they do it?" I did this when my kids were five and eight, and *wow,* was I blown away at how much I was doing for them. Within one month they were feeding the dogs, loading the dishwasher, cleaning their own rooms (or not), making their lunches for school, and doing light housework.

Here's the key, they didn't do any of it as well as I did, but I had to be okay with it. Hold here for a second; *you really need to be okay with it.* And why wouldn't you be? Some friend might stop by and see dog kibble spilled on the floor? They might see a messy bedroom? Or, god forbid, a dishwasher loaded improperly.

Who cares? Why is any of that important to us in the big scheme of things?

Let it go and let them grow.

Now let's look at another area, the time you spend at every practice/class/game/competition/parent meeting/school party/field trip and *driving* to them. *Of course* we don't have time for anything else in our lives!

Let me give you a great metaphor: Think of yourself as a glass pitcher full of water. Every day you are pouring yourself into everyone else, but you never stop to refill yourself. Is it any wonder you lose your temper, get frustrated, snap at people, or even worse, don't have time for your relationship with your spouse or significant other? Here comes the guilt . . . .

About the time I started giving my kids responsibilities, I realized they were at that age when they'll demand *all* our time if we don't set boundaries. Yes, that's what kids do.

While they were little, I worked a lot. Six days a week, 60 hours or more every week. I was blessed to be able to bring them to work with me. They played on my office floor and found many "aunties" and "uncles" within my pool of co-workers.

Things were relatively calm and on a manageable schedule until school and activities entered the picture. That's when all hell broke loose. I was still working the same schedule, but now had so much more to juggle and so many more self-imposed expectations. I barely had enough time to take a shower.

This went on for about three years. My daughters kept asking me to spend more time with them, so I shaved down my hours to a typical 9-5 day, picking them up at 5:15. School was over at 3:30, and the after-school program was outside on the playground. They got to play with their friends for almost two hours, which they (and I) thought was great.

When the after-school program shifted to keeping them stone-cold quiet, doing their homework in the cafeteria, my kids wanted to come home right at 3:30. I obliged. Then they wanted me to stop working on Saturdays. I obliged. Then they wanted me to stop taking the one business trip a month I always took. I obliged. Then they wanted me to show up at school for every class party, field trip, pep rally, practice, game, performance etc. I obliged.

Right about then I asked myself, "When will they get enough of my time?" The answer, unfortunately, is *never*.

Kids are kids, and they don't understand anything about boundaries. They learn very early exactly how to push our guilt buttons. You need to be the adult and set the boundaries; don't let your children erase them by pushing those buttons. Setting limits and saying "no" doesn't make you a bad mom.

Now, did I need to shave off some of my work hours? Yes. But my daughters wouldn't have stopped until I had given up a career that I loved dearly and helped provide a roof over their head, food on the table and a private Christian school education.

You need to understand this, especially those of you who are stay-at-home moms. It's even harder for you, because no one truly understands how much work is involved in running a household.

Your kids need to know beyond a shadow of a doubt

that you love them; they just *don't* need your every waking breath devoted to their comfort and happiness. Children thrive on a little adversity early in their lives; they become stronger as they learn to cope. Remember my grandfather? Keep him in mind the next time you start to feel guilty.

So, how do you defuse the Mommy guilt landmine?

First, set down a schedule that leaves time for you to pursue your own calling and purpose, whether it's your career, school, or even getting out of the dang house if you are a stay at home mom. Remember, your energy and love are the water in your pitcher. After pouring yourself into people all day, you must replenish that water. Doing things that you love and enjoy is how you replenish yourself. You can't pour your energy and love into the people you care most about if you are always empty.

Once you have set that schedule, now take a look at how you can enjoy or make use of "lost time." Lost time is the time driving them around, waiting for classes and practices to be over, etc., and I had a *ton* of it. I started figuring out how I could have a little fun while they were having theirs.

My first step was to take classes where my girls did. I'd been a dancer my whole life, but I gave it up after having kids because I had no time. When my daughters started taking dance classes, I sat in the waiting room for a month before it finally dawned on me to check for a class I might enjoy. At this point I hadn't danced in ten years, was 35 pounds overweight, and would be taking the class with a bunch of teenagers.

It would have been so easy to just sit and do nothing. Thank God that something in me was so desperate to get back to dancing that I was able to put my ego and my pride aside and join the class.

The first few months, I was embarrassingly bad, but again, *who cares!* I stayed in the back corner and made a mess of things, but I was having fun and being challenged. I was also losing weight and getting healthier. I hate going to the gym but love going to dance class.

The best part though, was how I was with my family when I got home. I was *happy!* I hugged more, I laughed more, nothing bothered me, I didn't snap at my husband and kids over stupid little things.

Fast forward to today. At 49, I'm in better shape than I was at 35, healthy, and on a competitive hip hop dance team—a team that just took third place overall at the Dallas Hip Hop Fest, which attracts all the best teams from around the country. Dance has been a major contribution to my overall happiness and well-being. (*Thank you*, Fenton Fulgham and FDF Dance Studio.)

When they took horseback riding lessons, so did I.

When they took ice skating lessons, I strapped on skates and had some fun. When they did things like soccer that didn't interest me or which I couldn't do alongside my daughters, I read a book. When was the last time you let yourself do that? If you don't like to read, watch something on Netflix that *you* want to watch. When was the last time *you* had control of the remote?

This reminds me of a funny scene in the movie *Date Night* with Tina Fey. Her husband is worried that she's fantasizing about another man (Mark Wahlberg, who wouldn't!), and Tina busts into a rant about her deepest, darkest fantasy: To go to a hotel for the weekend, sleep in, get room service, and read a great book in silence without any disruptions. Ha, I can relate, can you? When she gave her rant, she sounded like a truly empty vessel that needed to be refilled.

When was the last time you took a weekend just for you and your spouse or significant other? If you have family or close personal friends whom you trust and who love your kids, then you have no excuse. Will they feed them junk food? Probably. Let them watch stuff on TV that you wouldn't? Yep. Lighten up, a lifetime in our homogenized little world doesn't serve our kids.

It's great for children to see how other people live and function in their own worlds. Many times, the experience will make them appreciate their own lives more. Most important, they'll gain an understanding that not everyone is like them or thinks like them or does things like them—*and that's okay!* If they're in a safe and loving environment *relax* and go have some fun, *guilt free!*

> **Realize that how you do anything is how you do everything.**

Let's move on to some practical things that create guilt in your day. Don't over-promise and under-deliver; it's bad in business and even worse with your family. We've already discussed how this could break trust in the workplace, and in a family your children and your spouse need to know you're going to follow through.

The biggest key here is to *not* overcommit or forget what you committed to. I was the worst with this. My kids would ask me something while I was busy doing ten other things, and I would say "*Yes!*" without writing it down. When the day came and I dropped the ball, a rush of guilt came flooding in.

Thankfully, with smart phones you can quickly set a reminder, but you *must* do it. At the end of your day, note it in your calendar so that you can check for conflicts. This isn't a hard thing to do, but that's also why it often doesn't get done.

Realize that how you do *anything* is how you do *everything*. You'd make sure you wouldn't forget an appointment or a task at work or with people outside your family, so don't forget at home. Your family deserves your respect, too.

When you put this new commitment into your calendar, you get a chance to see how it fits into your life. If you realize you have a crazy week and you'll be too exhausted with everything else you have going on, just say "no." Your kids won't want you there if you're frazzled and cranky anyway. See if dad, grandma, or "auntie" can be there for them instead.

Another important step is to apologize to your children when you screw up. You will lose their respect if you expect them to apologize when they're wrong, but you never do. It's tough for us to admit when we're wrong; we don't want people to think less of us or figure out we don't know what the heck we are doing and that we're just doing the very best we can. It's okay—they love you and they will love you even more when you own up to your mistakes.

If you are frustrated with your landscaper, but yell at your children instead, apologize. When you're late picking them up, apologize. Granted, they are little, but they are people, too, and they deserve your respect. Apologizing when you mess up doesn't show children you are weak or incompetent; it shows them that you're human, and you love them enough to feel badly when you let them down.

An apology also allows children to learn how to forgive. The key is that once you have apologized and they have forgiven you, let it go and don't feel guilty.

One of the most helpful strategies I incorporated was "quittin' time." I realized that every night I was on mom duty all the way up to the minute that I finally collapsed into bed and shut my eyes. Every human needs about an hour to decompress before going to sleep. When you rob yourself of this time, your sleep and therefore your whole next day can be affected.

I put quittin' time into effect when my kids were obviously old enough to understand and comply; I think they were seven and ten. I should have started earlier with the 10-year-old but it's so challenging to keep things equal with sisters. They are always watching to make sure they are getting their fair share (hmmmm, maybe another landmine).

Before quittin' time began, I gave everyone in the house notice: "In one week and from then on, I'm off the clock at 9:30pm. Anything you need, you'll need to get it yourself after 9:30. That includes help with homework. Want a snack? Water? Help finding your tennis shoes for practice the next day? Want me to wash your basketball uniform that you forgot to put in the laundry and now it stinks to high heaven and your game is tomorrow? *Nope.*"

This was going to be my time to relax, catch up with my husband, watch a little TV other than the Disney channel, you get the picture.

My oldest was notorious for not checking what homework was due until right before bedtime. Usually she had an idea about what was due and it would be done on time, but every couple of weeks at 9:30 or 10:00 she'd discover she had more, and we'd have chaos. No more.

The first few weeks there was lots of whining, but then they realized I wasn't budging and they complied. My home became serene and peaceful every night at 9:30 because my girls were settled in with their stuff done. Did they go to school with two different socks, a dirty uniform, a missing homework assignment? Yes, and I was okay with that; the problems were short-lived. My daughters are better adults now because they learned self-sufficiency early.

My most effective guilt-control strategy is how I decided to handle the time immediately after I picked my children up from school or walked in from work— the time of day that mommy guilt is at its peak. That's when we're winding down our workday and making those last couple calls or sending that last email, and it's also when our kids want our full, undivided attention.

Let me tell you, they deserve our complete focus. You haven't seen them for hours and they have lots to talk to you about and share, and you want to encourage that communication. This strategy will save you lots of heartache.

First, finish the call or the email *before* you pick up your kids or walk into the house. I can't tell you how many times I parked around the corner from their school or sat in the garage to finish a call. When you walk in, be *fully* present and focused on your kids. Plan on 20-30 minutes of focused love and attention (don't you *dare* pick up your phone or start doing something domestic). Get down on the ground and play with them, sit on the couch and talk, engage them. You'll be shocked to learn that kids have a short attention span (whoops—a little sarcasm here), and in 20-30 minutes they'll pretty much be bored with you and want to go do something else.

Now, let's look at what happens in most households. Mom picks the kids up, and she is on and off the phone. When she walks in the door, she goes straight to making dinner, lunches for the next day, laundry, etc., and all the while the kids are underfoot vying for her attention: *Mom! Mom! Mom!* The first 20-30 minutes home is stressful, frustrating, and guilt-producing until finally the kids give up and flip on the TV.

If you just focus on your children and your relationship with them for that small window of time, things will be *so* much better for you and your kids.

I know we've spent a lot of time on this topic, but mommy guilt is destructive in every way to you and your kids. Is there such a thing as the perfect mom?

No, we do the very best we can for our children, pray a lot, work on our patience, try to keep them safe despite themselves and their curiosity in how an electric socket works, all the while we keep them fed and as clean as possible.

Children don't come with an owner's manual, and since they all have completely different souls, advice from friends and books is limited.

So, here's my last piece of advice:

Love fiercely, laugh often, and pray for God's wisdom and protection. It's also a good idea to watch the movie *Bad Moms* at least once a month to remind yourself that you're not *that* bad!

CHAPTER SEVEN

LANDMINE: COMPARISON

Comparison will cause you to either feel prideful or depressed, but never *fulfilled.*

—Lisa Bevere

Defusing the comparison landmine is easy! Stop looking at social media, reading gossip and fashion magazines, and for goodness sakes, stay far away from Pinterest. If you can't look at Facebook or Instagram without feeling a nagging, gnawing sensation of guilt or feeling like you're "less than," stay off them. Post important pics that you want family to see and immediately close the app.

You have to understand that everyone, including you, posts things in a positive light. Social media and the mainstream media have very little to do with "reality;" even reality TV is scripted and very rarely close to what really happens.

I saw a friend's post on Facebook the other day of her beautiful family sitting in a field of flowers with huge smiles on their faces and the sun creating a halo effect around all of them, mom and dad's hands sweetly resting on their children's shoulders. It was breathtaking. But . . . I happened to be there when that picture was taken.

It was chaos, tears from the little ones, whines from the older ones, a frustrated photographer, a sullen, angry dad and a screaming mother. I called her after I saw the post and we had a great laugh about it. But how many of you, not knowing the behind-the-scenes story, would have been depressed by the perfect post?

Or worse yet, what do we put our family through to ensure our outward persona reeks of perfection? This comparison landmine feeds and re-plants our insecurity landmine and causes us to be petty and catty. This is really a three-headed landmine that can do an immense amount of damage in our relationships, both at work and at home.

One of the quickest ways to destroy relationships is with the monster we become when we try to keep up with the Joneses: We spend money we shouldn't, we spread gossip about someone we feel inferior to, we push, pull, and prod our families incessantly to do things they don't want to do. Soon, we look in the mirror and don't even recognize the face staring back at us. How many times have you ruined a perfectly good moment because you had to get the "perfect" picture or the meal had to be "perfect" or your outfit needed to be "perfect"?

I can remember a wedding that illustrates my point.

I was not in the wedding party, but I was a close enough friend to be around during much of the planning. The bride had everything researched, pinned, and planned. There was nothing she hadn't thought of and there were tons of moving pieces—not just the church and reception venue, flowers, dress, attendants, and menu like most weddings. She'd planned about 20-30 extra touches.

Well, I'm sure you can see where this is going. On the big day, everything was going along as planned until we got to the reception. Something didn't happen, something minor that wasn't even a special touch to make the day more special for her and her new husband. It was a small thing, just for the guests, and it didn't affect the event in any way, but it didn't go as planned. *KaBoom!* Landmine detonated with debris everywhere, all over the perfect reception.

The bride had let herself get *so* wrapped up in having the perfect wedding, one designed to outdo everyone else's, that when something inevitably went wrong, the pressure was too much. She blew up in the middle of the event, all over everyone. Seriously, no one would have even known it was supposed to happen if she hadn't been so upset.

She ruined her big moment, a moment she can never get back, her husband can never get back, and for what? Now, I know brides are already under a great deal of stress just because of the huge decision that they're making, but they do themselves a huge disservice by trying to live up to social pressure for the perfect wedding day. Silly brides, right?

Let's pause for a second and ask when was the last time *we* lost our temper because something or someone didn't live up to our expectation(s) they had no idea even existed? "Why can't you be as romantic as Julie's husband?;" "Why don't you dress like Susan's husband, he always looks so handsome?;" "Why don't you get good grades like your sister?;" "Why can't I be thin, beautiful, youthful, tan, pale, blond, brunette, younger, older, more talented, etc., etc., etc.?"

There is scientific research from the Institute of Psychiatry in London that proves the longer a woman stares in the mirror, the more dissatisfied she becomes with her looks. Even the most beautiful women I've met are always finding flaws and faults in their faces and bodies. I've even been guilty of doing this, knowing full well the damage I'm doing to my self-esteem, and worse yet, to those around me.

There is no such thing as a perfect person on this earth; there hasn't been for more than 2,000 years. You will drive yourself and everyone around you insane until you defuse this landmine, ladies.

The men in our lives rarely struggle with this the way we women do. They might find motivation in the workplace to work harder through comparison-inspired competition, but rarely do they become catty or petty. Some do, but most just aren't wrapped up in what everyone else thinks about them like we are.

For some of you, defusing the comparison landmine will be as easy as getting off social media. Delete the apps from your phone so you're not tempted to browse when you have a few minutes. Be crazy and do a cold-turkey social media "fast" for 30 days, meaning don't even open a social media app for *any* reason.

Notice how great you feel.

When I was struggling with food allergies, my doctor told me to fast for 48 hours and then add one new food back into my diet at a time. If I felt great but then became sluggish and bloated right after eating, I had just consumed the culprit.

See how you feel taking 30 days away from social media. Don't just stop with social media, do a fast from anything that causes you to spiral into comparison-inspired insecurity. For some of you it's fashion or gossip magazines; for others it's TV programs on HGTV or other home improvement networks, or apps like Pinterest, or that one friend that's uber creative. Take a break from *whatever* feeds your insecurities.

Once you've removed the steady bombardment of comparison messages implying that you need to be more/do more, rest for 30 days. Spend some time realizing *you are enough*.

> *Either change the people around you, or change the people around you.*

Do you have room for improvement? Of course! Don't ever stop learning and growing, but don't overwhelm yourself. Don't use comparisons to choose your targets.

After 30 days, slowly start adding in what you removed.

Can you handle Facebook and *People* magazine, but then when you throw Pinterest back in the mix you start to feel anxious? Monitor what enhances your day and what pushes you into unhealthy, stressful, harmful, comparison.

Maybe it's the people in your day-to-day life that are causing you this type of stress. If the people around you don't love and appreciate you, then there is another quote I want to give you: *Either change the people around you, or change the people around you.* Re-read that a few times so that you really understand whom you're striving to please. My daily purpose is to please God, then myself and family, and really it stops there.

I have no control over what people think about me.

One of my mentors gave me another great quote: *If you like me or not is your decision; if you respect me, that's my decision.* Beyond that, I let it go. Stop trying to fill the void of insecurity with your ego. It will never be enough. It's time to look in the mirror and fall in love with that precious beauty staring back at you.

CHAPTER EIGHT

LANDMINE:
DOUBT

This is what I want . . .well, what do you think, am I crazy? Should I? Shouldn't I? No, seriously, I need your help. What's your honest opinion?

And this is just us trying to order from the Cheesecake Factory menu for lunch! We women are the epitome of second guessers. There is a time for debate and there is a time for decision. Why, oh why, my sisters, do we have such a hard time making a decision, and, even more importantly, sticking to it?

Some of you career women have mastered the art of making decisions and following through at work, but let's take a moment to evaluate *all* areas of our lives. You might be strong and decisive in the boardroom, but the Cheesecake Factory example is you at lunch. Personally, I have defused this landmine a long time ago, and indecisiveness is flat irritating to me, especially if I'm the one doing it.

For some of you, it's still your fallback decision-making mode. You need to realize that constantly second-guessing yourself helps re-plant many of the other landmines.

For others, it's even worse: The doubt begins from the moment you wake up to the moment you fall asleep:

What should I wear? Do I look fat? Boom!

What should I eat? Should I eat? Boom!

I wonder if my boss was just having a bad day or if he was irritated with me for something? Boom!

Did they intentionally not invite me to happy hour? Boom!

I wonder if my presentation was good enough? Boom!

Did they ask me to leave the meeting so they could talk about me? Boom!

This is the second time this week my husband is working late, is he upset with me for something? Boom!

You get the picture.

What you might not fully understand is that detonating this landmine over and over again all day long permanently damages you. There's destruction every time a landmine detonates.

Doubt becomes a destructive habit.

What if your boss asks you a question in a meeting? Will you answer with confidence or sound unsure and shaky? If you can never make a decision, your work friends will stop asking you to go out. If you can't make up your mind about your wardrobe or which way you should get to work, you'll soon get in trouble for being late on a consistent basis. When you feel unsure of your performance at work, you'll start to pester people to reassure and compliment you.

Confidence is one of the *most* attractive attributes of every human being, including you! Look at all the musicians, athletes, artists, businessmen, leaders, and even actors who aren't drop-dead gorgeous but who definitely grab our attention. They are confident and it's sexy!

In order to defuse our doubt landmine, we have to trace our way back to major events that caused us to doubt ourselves. Then discover the areas where we are still confident, so that we can help that confidence spill over into *all* areas of our lives.

First, let's think back to your first memory of doubting yourself. Did a parent scream at you for a bad decision, a friend laugh at you for a bad hair day, or a teacher humiliate you in front of the entire class? Most of us can't remember much about our childhoods, but we usually can remember super highs and super lows. So, take a minute and think of what stands out . . . .

As adults, most of us look back at our childhood and say, *Oh, that was no big deal, I'm so not affected by that*, or *I'm over it*. Unfortunately, that's not the truth. We as humans learn during high emotion. It's a trait that served us well in prehistoric times when we needed to avoid lurking predators, but it can really trip us up in our modern, day-by-day environment. Put yourself back into your past—remember your traumatic moments, not as a mature adult, but as a scared little child, embarrassed kid, or brokenhearted teen.

Take this chance to really be in the moment and watch yourself in the experience. You need to understand that you were young, and probably fast to act and slow to think, like every young person. We can't replay past insecurities and doubts from when we were young without including the perspective and the wisdom we now possess.

And *yes*, you possess this wisdom: *The wisdom to know what you know, know what you like, and know who you are.*

There are a great many things that I don't know and still need to learn, but those three things I do know. These three phrases boil down to not caring what people think about anything we do.

Do I ask advice from respected mentors, consult God, and review my conscience? As I said before, yes! Beyond that, it comes down to those three questions.

I know what I know. I know how to dance; I know how to raise kids; I know how to lead a team; I know how to deliver a message in front of a crowd of over 10,000 people.

You know, too. Take five minutes and write down a list of the things you *know*.

Now, how about the things you know you *like*?

This was hard for me to answer until just recently. My life was focused on wanting to please everyone around me and do everything they liked for so long that I failed to keep tabs on what was important to me. Not to worry, I figured it out, and you can too.

What worked for me was keeping a list in my phone of the things and activities that I liked or wanted to do. Whenever I thought of something, I'd add it to the list, and before long I had quite a long list! It was incredibly exciting to start doing, going, eating, and playing all the things on that list. Because of my list, I've traveled to India, Cuba, amazing national parks right here in the States, and have had incredible adventures and life experiences with friends and family. So get busy on your list.

Finally, know who you *are*. Now, this is where you need to be brutally honest with yourself. If you don't know who you are, you will end up pretending to be someone that you're not.

So many women tell me they don't know how to be a good friend. Well, don't you think that might be important to share with your friends? Instead, most women will act like a good friend, but when push comes to shove and they need to step up in support of a friend, they blow it. They don't know what they don't know. If you're honest with your friends, they will understand—remarkably!—and sometimes teach you a thing or two.

Get busy on this list; I'll even get you started. Circle which applies most to you in each set:

I tend to be:

Giving/selfish

A great listener/a talker

Thoughtful/forgetful

Kind/sarcastic

Punctual/late

Neat/messy

Truthful/a truth bender

Energy giver/energy sucker

Passive/aggressive (or even worse, passive-aggressive

Introverted/extroverted

Supporter/problem finder

Victor/victim

Positive/negative

Now, I know you would all love to circle all the positives but you need to be honest with yourself. If you're not, you will set yourself up to fail, and ultimately you'll keep doubting yourself.

> *Surround yourself with people who celebrate you, not tolerate you.*

The doubt landmine is hard to defuse because it boils down to a single cause: We want to please everyone around us. As we've already discussed, this is a recipe for disaster. Remember your mother saying, "You can't please all the people all the time?"

It's true—and why would you want to, anyway? You'll spend your precious energy and joy trying to make people happy who just don't want to be.

Surround yourself with people who celebrate you, not tolerate you; people who feed your joy; and people who help you stretch and grow. Choose people you can be yourself with *all* the time. Doesn't that sound fantastic? Of course it does. The problem is, most of you have accumulated a large number of "friends" and acquaintances who like your fake self.

When you step out and start being real and authentic, some so-called friends won't like hanging around you anymore. That's ok! Don't panic! There are 326 million people in the United States and over seven billion on the planet; you will find new friends! Especially if you have eradicated all the landmines we've previously discussed, people will be dying to hang out with you!

You build others up, you're confident, you're decisive, you don't gossip or belittle people behind their backs—you sound pretty amazing, don't you?

Focus on being the person you would love to have as a friend, and you'll be amazed by the wonderful people you begin to attract into your life.

CHAPTER NINE

LANDMINE: OVEREMOTIONAL

H ere's another awesome quote: *If you don't educate your emotions, they'll embarrass you.*

How many of us can tell story upon story of times we let our emotions run wild and get the best of us? I struggled for years throughout my late teens and early twenties with runaway emotions. When I was frustrated, angry, embarrassed, or sad, I'd start to cry. Not a great trait to be remembered for when you're trying to build a successful business and gain trust and respect in the boardroom. We women, *much* more so than men, wear our emotions on our sleeves. This often has negative consequences.

One of the biggest keys to controlling our emotions is to control our thoughts.

When our emotions are high, our logic is usually low, and that's *never* a good combination. I was in a board meeting early in my career that switched rapidly from a professional debate into a vicious attack. The venom wasn't even directed at me but at my team leader.

I had so much I wanted to say in his defense (*someone* had to), but I could feel the emotion welling up in my throat, and it took everything I could muster to keep from crying. I knew if I said one word, the dam would break. I was very aware of my team leader's composure; it amazed me that as he sat there, the target of an undeserving attack, he was as calm and cool as when he walked into the room. I was shocked, flabbergasted, and, quite frankly, jealous! How did he maintain his composure under such horrible circumstances?

> *Your thoughts determine your emotions.*

A few weeks later, everything had been sorted out and I finally had the courage to ask him how he managed. He taught me an invaluable lesson that day: He explained that our emotions are directly tied to our thoughts. He said "Kelly, if someone called you a drug addict, would you go into a tirade defending yourself? No, because you *know* you're not a drug addict. Your thoughts determine your emotions, so when someone says or does something horrible to you, it is up to *you* to keep the right thinking."

The key for us women is to *not* speak before we get our emotions "in check." *Breathe*; count to ten; visualize yourself in your "happy place" or whichever clichéd technique works for you. This works!

Personally, I pray. Whichever you decide upon as

your go-to strategy doesn't matter; what matters is that you give yourself time to collect your thoughts and make sure they're free of reckless, unchecked emotion.

That doesn't mean you can't feel emotion; emotion is fine, even helpful. Reckless, unchecked emotion, on the other hand, is not contained; it's the kind of emotion that causes us to say things we regret or things that we just flat out shouldn't have said. As bad as the repercussions can be in our career world, it can be even more damaging with our family and friends.

When we have a great deal of respect for someone, we tend to treat them *very* well. We buy them lunch, joyfully help them with things, even laugh at jokes that aren't funny. As we get to know someone well and start developing deeper trust, we also become more aware of their faults. Unfortunately, it tends to be the case that as trust increases, respect usually decreases; despite our good intentions, we begin to treat the people closest to us very differently.

There was a time in my life that I felt completely and utterly overwhelmed. I had landmines blowing up all day, every day, and just didn't know what to do. I was seven months pregnant with our second child. My husband was on the road working as much as possible so he could spend a chunk of time at home when the baby arrived. He was only home one or two days every three weeks, and I was exhausted. Working full-time, managing the household finances, cooking, cleaning, and taking care of a strong-willed three-year-old (hats off to all my single moms out there!)—I was exhausted *all* day, *every* day.

As I grew bigger and bigger and more uncomfortable; my patience grew smaller and smaller. One night, our three-year-old just wouldn't go to bed. It had been a really long and exhausting day, and I needed to forgo all my domestic duties for the night so I could pour myself into bed early. I picked up fast food for my daughter and ignored the dirty dishes and the laundry. I was finally going to get a solid nights' sleep! After dinner and a bath, I went to put her to bed at 9:00, hoping to be in bed myself by 9:30.

Well, after she stalled for two hours and then got out of bed to play in the family room whenever I went to my room, I lost it, **BAM,** landmine detonated! To this day I have never lost my temper as badly—not even *close* to as badly—as I lost it that night. I can only imagine the terrifying expression on my face as I came unglued, and the pitch and tone of my voice was surely something from a horror movie.

She was so terrified that she flinched whenever I said her name for three weeks. It took at least two months for her to trust me again emotionally. I learned a very valuable and painful lesson about the importance of controlling my emotions.

I hate to take you to a negative place, but it's for your own good. There isn't a woman reading this that can honestly say that she hasn't scared herself by losing her temper in a horrible way with either her kids or her spouse. For some of us it happened a handful of times; others, a couple of times a year; others, a few times a month; unfortunately for some, it may be a few times a week.

What is your identity within your family?

Not to worry, I have a strategy that will definitely help: Think of a person that you immensely respect (a mentor, past or present; a friend of the family you never wanted to say or do something stupid in front of; a past teacher whom you truly loved and respected). Now, the next time you are about to lose control and completely lose it in front of your family or anyone you love, I want you to visualize that well-respected person standing right next to the person at the receiving end of your tirade.

Would you ever speak to that person the way you're speaking to your family member or friend? Of course not! So, *stop* in your tracks, apologize and take a minute to regroup.

Just because they love you and will forgive you, it's not acceptable to let your emotions override your decency and kindness.

This doesn't mean you should replant a guilt landmine. You didn't know better, now you do. Work on getting control of your emotions every day and with practice, you will become master of this beast.

Remember, the key to truly controlling our emotions lies in controlling our thoughts. What truly controls our thoughts happens to be one of *the* most dangerous landmines, *negative self-talk*.

CHAPTER TEN

LANDMINE: NEGATIVE SELF-TALK

M ost of you would *never* let someone else talk to you the way you talk to yourself!

Evidence is conclusive that your self-talk has a direct bearing on your performance.—Zig Ziglar

Don't be a victim of negative self-talk—remember you *are listening.*—Bob Proctor

He who would be useful, strong, and happy must cease to be a passive receptacle for the negative, beggarly, and impure streams of thought.—James Allen

The inner speech, your thoughts, can cause you to be rich or poor, loved or unloved, attractive or unattractive, powerful or weak.—Ralph Charell.

This is just a tiny sample of the thousands of quotes you can find on Google about self-talk.

Self-talk goes on in your brain when you're awake, asleep, and halfway in between. It can go both directions: It can be positive and give you strength and courage, or it can drag you down, even down and out. It's not just a good idea to monitor our inner dialogue and change it when necessary, according to these experts and hundreds of others—*it's a must!*

The negative self-talk landmine is absolutely connected to *every single* landmine we've already discussed.

And here's the really bad news: Negative self-talk can automatically reset any of the landmines you've already defused. Imagine defusing victim mentality, gossiping, backstabbing, mommy guilt, and comparison landmines (congratulations!). Then all it takes is one negative internal conversation with yourself, and *all of them are reset!* Months of hard work are down the drain, and now you must go back and start defusing them all over again.

Take a big breath. Dream for a moment that you wanted to create a private retreat within your house, a pristine white room: It has white walls with pale artwork, a beautiful, lush white carpet, white marble fireplace with fragrant white flowers in crystal vases everywhere, and a gorgeous, plush white couch in the center. Go ahead, close your eyes and picture it.

Now imagine it's yours—your dream room! You saved and saved for years, ripped pictures from magazines, hired a designer. It's finally done. Your dream is now your reality for you to enjoy.

The next morning as you brew your coffee, you're bouncing with anticipation, filled with desire to go sit in your beautiful new room and breathe in the peace and beauty. The pot's finally ready; you pour your coffee into a spill-proof cup, and head into your sanctuary. As you carefully push the door open, the stench hits you first.

When I began consciously directing my morning self-talk to be positive, things turned around immediately.

Your nostrils stinging, you walk in and see the horror! Someone has spread at least ten barrels of dog poop all over the room. To add insult to injury, the filth is rubbed into the upholstery and carpet and smeared all over the walls.

You drop your coffee cup and run full speed to the computer that records security camera footage of every room in the house to discover *who* could've done this to you, *who* destroyed your dream?

As you scroll back through the footage, you see the culprit. As you hit pause and stare closely at her face, a huge lump fills your throat. *It's you!*

Now let's be clear, the beautiful white room is your mind, and the dog poop is negative self-talk.

The Bible says we get a fresh batch of joy every

morning. For about two years, I must have forgotten this wonderful news, because I got up stressed, angry, and sad almost every day.

Thankfully, because I'd been teaching this topic for over a decade, I finally realized I needed to check myself and take inventory of my self-talk. Bingo!

Though I was very effective at directing my self-talk during the day, I discovered I had lost conscious control of those first 10-20 minutes when I woke up, when I was half-sleep, half awake. That was when I started to think about all the problems I was going to face that day, the hurts I had endured the day before, and wondered if I had the strength to tackle my day. My self-talk was totally negative.

I was blown away! That's not me! I know better!

Sure enough, with conscious reflection, I realized when I opened my eyes I *was* happy and full of hope and joy. When I began consciously directing my morning self-talk to be positive, things turned around immediately. I spoke words of encouragement, love and power to myself, expressed gratitude for all the blessings that I had at that moment (some days my list was as short as "my kids and I can see, walk, and breathe"), and prayed for my loved ones struggling with their own set of problems. My joy was preserved and protected.

Depression and suicide both thrive inside the negative self-talk landmine, and that's why it is *so* important to constantly be searching your minefield for this particularly dangerous mine.

Self-talk creates a snowball effect much quicker than any of the other mines we've discussed. There is no such place as *neutral*; your internal dialogue keeps you mentally spiraling either downward or upward.

For years, I've worked with people struggling with depression. Early on, I found one of the most effective actions they could take was to volunteer for organizations helping the less fortunate. Examples

Faith it 'til you make it.

guaranteed to inspire most include a children's cancer ward filled with mini-warriors, a retirement home full of forgotten people who just need human love and connection, and a food pantry for single moms who are struggling every week just to put food on the table.

Your own gratitude and thankfulness create the foundation for healthy, positive self-talk. If you are a spiritual person, faith and hope are an essential part of the mix.

Back in the day, there was a saying for someone trying to do something for the first time, "Fake it 'til you make it."

My dear friend Kimberly Bliquez introduced me to an even better version that I love: "*Faith* it 'til you make it." By this, Kimberly means that we have to have faith in a desired outcome *before* that outcome can come to reality. You must take the first action in faith.

Anyone can have a great day when everything is going perfectly and they're feeling confident. But when we are in the middle of a storm, only those of us who can speak with faith that everything will work out (and continue to direct our internal dialogue in an upward, positive direction) will come out with our joy intact.

When you first start saying positive things about yourself, it will feel *very* strange. Relax, you're all alone where no one can hear you. I recommend that you stand in your bathroom with the door closed, looking directly at yourself in the mirror.

What do you say?

First, make a list of "*I am*" statements. I'll share mine with you to get you started; feel free to steal any and all of them. (Truly, though, you need to spend some time thinking about *your* positive attributes.)

I am:

Chosen

Loved

Redeemed

Righteous because of Him

Playful

Beautiful

Social

Faithful

Loyal

Encouraging

Obedient to God's will for my life

Intelligent

Fun

Adventurous

Loving

Independent

Strong-willed

Strong-minded

After I tell myself all of these positive things, I end with my marching orders for the day. Again, I'll share mine (careful, though, don't replant your offendable landmine because of my language):

Serve people, dream big, and be a *bad ass!*

Now that you've started your day on a high note, you must actively monitor what you say both internally and out loud all day.

How many of us have heard our friends practice bad self-talk? They tear themselves down during a conversation, they say they'll catch the bug going around, or predict the worst possible outcome to what they're about to do. Guess what, you do it too. We *all* do.

I know better and I *still* catch myself with negative self-talk after twenty-plus years of coaching people *not* to do it. Several times a week, I'll catch myself saying, "I

> *I would love to see your list if you feel comfortable sharing it with the world. The act of declaring it publicly is very positive and will help you keep more accountable to your real self.*
>
> *Quick, grab your phone and go to my Facebook fan page @kellymathewsaccetta (be careful not to post on my personal page; your post won't show up), and post your list. If you aren't on Facebook, visit my website www.truth.coach and send me an email. At least I will know and that will help you stay true to you!*

have a slow metabolism," "I'm overwhelmed," "I don't have enough time" . . . and that's just the start.

We all need to be constantly vigilant. Don't say anything negative about yourself, *you* are listening. Your subconscious doesn't run on logic; it believes whatever you tell it!

Again, the opposite is true. If you say positive things, your subconscious will believe those words, too. Just feed your brain the internal dialogue whenever you were about to say something negative about yourself.

If you were about to say out loud, "I have a slow metabolism," instead consciously and positively tell yourself the reverse: "I'm so thankful that my body burns through my food like a blast furnace."

If you were going to complain, "I'm so over-whelmed," instead say internally, "I'm glad that I plan my days *so* well that I can handle the pressure even when I get more than expected."

My go-to positive statement is one of my favorite bible verses:

I can do all things through him who strengthens me. (Philippians 4:13, *English Standard Version*)

You get the point. Be ultra careful of what you say to yourself and about yourself at all times. It's hard work at first, and you'll be sporadic throughout the day; but you'll get better as you keep practicing. You must be intentional about positive self-talk; it will have much more of an impact in your life if you use it regularly, not just occasionally.

The odds are, you've been telling your subconscious the same negative garbage for decades. While you need to replace this trash with positive self-talk, *repetition* is what will make the real difference within our subconscious.

Thankfully, I am surrounded by family, friends, and associates who also understand this concept and take it to heart. We keep each other pointed in the right direction, and we never hesitate to say, "Don't say that to yourself" whenever one of us has a moment of weakness. Who do you surround yourself with? Hmmm. It makes a difference.

This introduces a key to positive self-talk. Who *do* you spend time with? Do they lift you up or tear you down?

Don't get me wrong, I'm not saying you need to surround yourself at all times with peaceful, loving souls singing "Kumbaya." I love sarcasm, and a funny joke at my expense here and there. But, are you around people who do it constantly? Believe me or not, their actions have an effect on you.

Does a girlfriend do nothing but criticize everyone, including you? Does a parent make you the butt of every joke? Does your spouse love to point out your flaws and embarrass you in front of others?

Like I shared with you before, you need to *change the people around you, or change the people around you.* You need to have open and honest conversations with the people in your life, setting new boundaries of what's acceptable, or you need to find new people to hang out with.

Of course, first we need to get past the offendable landmine. Only then we can realize our internal dialog—what's triggered by someone's words—is the *real* reason we're offended or hurt. This goes back to everything we have discussed thus far, especially the need to know who you are and *whose* you are! (God don't make no junk.)

God blesses us all with the precious gift of life. Do

some of us take this gift and create a junky life through our selfishness and bad decisions? Yes, but that's not God's purpose or plan.

It's not his plan for you—you were uniquely created—so how can you ever compare yourself to others in this world and what they do? You don't look like anyone else, you don't act like anyone else, think like anyone else, feel like anyone else . . . .

So why in the world do you expect the world to understand exactly who you are? Why would you ever try to bend yourself in every direction to get the world's approval?

Conversely, you can't expect the world to bend to you, to your perspective, and to the set of rules and values you've adopted for *your* life. If someone thinks you don't look, act, speak, or do things the way *they* want, it's *their* opinion and they're entitled to it.

When someone gives their opinion, listen—just don't go into a total re-evaluation mode of your own core beliefs. We can learn something from everyone or anyone; sometimes the most valuable things we learn are what *not* to do or say. It's said that stupid people never learn from their mistakes, smart people learn from theirs, and wise people learn from the mistakes of others.

Why let anything *anyone* says make you have unhealthy, negative self-talk? I only care what a trusted and respected mentor says, or God himself, and then I listen to find how I might improve myself.

I've gotten to the point where people can like me, hate me, respect me, listen to me, or not. It doesn't hurt me, I don't give their negative chatter a second thought, and I don't need their compliments to feel good.

This is *huge* growth for me! Women like me who've struggled with issues of abandonment tend to try to please everyone so we won't be deserted again. It's a very real thing. I can't tell you how many times I stressed and worried about whether a friend was mad at me, or if people liked me, and I'd figuratively bend myself into a pretzel trying to please everyone.

When someone left my life, my self-talk about what I must have done to drive them away was truly an exercise in human self-torture. I finally realized that people are in our life for a reason, a season, or a lifetime.

Maybe it's time for you to relax and let go of people you've been clinging onto. If they truly love and value you, they will still be there when you start living the landmine-free version of your true self.

CHAPTER ELEVEN

LANDMINE: BITTERNESS AND UNFORGIVENESS

If our self-talk landmine is dangerous because it re-sets all the other landmines we've discussed, be aware: The double-headed landmine of bitterness and unforgiveness is *far* more dangerous. This monster not only re-sets all of our landmines, but it detonates them, too—sometimes all at the same time.

When we hold onto bitterness and unforgiveness, it pulls the trigger on insecurity, doubt, gossiping, two faced, cattiness, pettiness, being offendable, self-promotion, fear, guilt, comparison, defensiveness, jealousy, victim mentality, and of course, negative self-talk. *BAM!*

Even with all the trials and tribulations of my earlier years, somehow I managed to avoid planting this gigantic landmine for most of my life.

It only took root about two years ago, when I, like many of you, got dealt the ultimate rejection card. The man I had been with and loved for 26 years decided that, as much as he loved me as a person and a business partner, he was no longer "in love" with me.

I was devastated, broken, angry, hurt, confused; the list goes on and on. Our two children were grown, one out of the house, and one on her way to college. I looked at my life that had been so full of direction and purpose, and it was now empty, wiped clean.

Soon after my initial shock, I planted my bitterness and unforgiveness landmine, and it began to cause destruction in every area of my life.

Thankfully, I kept my bitterness to myself, and I only confided and shared it with two highly trained and highly trusted individuals, my therapist and my spiritual advisor.

Most of us women don't keep it to ourselves, unfortunately; we share too much with too many unqualified, untrained, and sometimes untrustworthy people.

As it's shared over and over, our bitterness and unforgiveness landmine gains even greater strength. Often, a friend or loved one whose heart is in the right place encourages us to "strike back" or "get even." Unfortunately, all that does is create even more destruction in our lives. All hate can ever breed is more hate, and now we've doomed ourselves to a cycle that is very hard to escape as it fans the flames of bitterness and unforgiveness.

As we start taking our friends' so-called advice and act out in destructive ways, all of the landmines begin to explode. Negative self-talk creates insecurity, and then gossiping. Then we post something we shouldn't on social media, and now we've detonated a slew of backstabbing mines. Someone will surely write a comment you take the wrong way and detonate your offendable and overemotional landmines. Then your negative self-talk kicks in again to help detonate victim mentality, insecurity, and doubt. Mommy guilt will be in there too, don't doubt it.

It circles around again, and again, and each spiral is more vicious. Truly, this can all happen in a matter of hours. We look around at the destruction and devastation *we* actually just caused, then blame it on the one who wronged us in the first place. Re-set, and bam; we start detonating them all over again.

The big question you have to ask yourself is this: *Who* is enduring most of the pain and damage? The person who left you, raped you, gave you up for adoption, molested you, stole from you? No, usually that person is long gone emotionally and or physically. The one who endures the damage is *you*, over and over and over, sometimes for decades, sometimes for a lifetime.

Bitterness and unforgiveness are not worth it! They don't serve you well, and they destroy your peace and joy. They also hold you back from ever finding your true purpose in life. You have to move past this place of self-centered pain and realize there might be people out there in the world counting on you for great things that never materialize because you are stuck in the mire of bitterness and unforgiveness.

If you don't know Oprah Winfrey's story, this is a good time to learn, because it's a perfect example of this situation. She was horribly abused as a young girl, and she could have easily remained stuck in bitterness. Instead, how many people have been inspired by Oprah herself and the various projects she has accomplished?

Maybe you're not Oprah, but maybe you could have an even greater impact than Oprah. Who knows what God has intended for your life's purpose? He and you certainly don't want you sitting paralyzed in a sea of destruction.

So how, oh *how* do you dismantle and remove such a dangerous weapon?

Forgiveness. We touched on this at the beginning of the book, but let's really dig in to our truth and realize it is the key.

As much hurt as my ex-husband's revelation caused, did I really want him to stay silent and in a loveless marriage for the rest of my life? Don't *I* deserve to be in a marriage with someone who's spectacularly amazing, who thinks *I'm* spectacularly amazing? Shouldn't my daughters see me show respect to the man who was truly the best father that they could have hoped for? Shouldn't my family and friends see an example of what love, peace, and joy in the middle of a shit storm really looks like?

And, speaking as a Christian to those of you who profess the faith, didn't Christ pay the ultimate price with His life so that we can have unconditional grace, mercy and forgiveness in our Father's eyes? Haven't we been forgiven for so much?

We need to forgive and forget, for once and for all.

To those of us who have just flat suffered undeservedly from rape, molestation, or all sorts of atrocities inflicted upon us, no matter *how* bad: *We need to forgive and forget, for once and for all.*

I know many of you have suffered through so much more than I have, and I am in no way trying to discount your pain by sharing mine. I share to give you a different perspective.

Over the years, I've learned that emotion is emotion, pain is pain. Sometimes I've encountered someone going through a tough time, and found myself saying inside my head, *"You're upset about that?"* I have to remind myself that her suffering is no less painful just because it's a problem that wouldn't faze me. We tend to forget that we are all on different journeys and God has blessed us with different gifts to guide us.

So, let's stop isolating ourselves in our pain, and realize we *all* deal with it *all* the time. You have sisters all around you who can relate and comfort you through your pain, even though they don't share your specific pain or issue.

My rape story is all too familiar. I was a brand-new college freshman, away from home only about three weeks, and like many freshmen, I'd been celebrating my brand-new freedom by partying. What I failed to realize is that I didn't have the safety net of my friends, my brothers, and my brothers' friends who had my back through high school. One night at a fraternity party, I realized I'd had too much to drink, and decided I would head home—alone.

I really didn't know where I was going because I had just arrived on campus, and I ended up cutting through a park. I saw a guy sitting on a picnic table smoking a cigarette, so as I went by, I stopped and asked him for one. We talked for a few minutes, and he said "Sure, I have more cigarettes, but they're in my house, across the street." He seemed harmless enough and was even sort of sweet, so I followed him across the street and in the door.

As the door closed, I heard an alarm going off in my hazy drunken brain, but I chose to ignore it. I thought, "I'm strong, athletic, invincible . . ." all the common thoughts in a teenage brain that's swimming in alcohol. He handed me the cigarette, and as I took it he kissed me. I said, "Thanks for the cigarette," and tried to turn to leave but his grip tightened and I was trapped.

Thankfully, I got out with my life and wasn't damaged too badly physically, but I was totally unaware of the emotional damage that I suffered. In my shame, I didn't speak about it to anyone for almost thirty years, until just a few years ago.

When I say that I *know* it's hard to forgive and let go, I really do understand. Even if my particular situation pales in comparison to what you went through, it doesn't make a difference when it comes to forgiveness. It's our only hope for peace and healing.

I forgave my rapist about ten years after it happened, when I heard a sermon about forgiveness. What I didn't realize for another twenty years is that I'd never forgiven myself. For decades, I held on to so much anger and bitterness towards myself and replayed the negative self-talk on an endless loop: *How could I have been so stupid? Why did I drink so much? Why did I leave the party alone? Why did I go into his* house?

Unfortunately, like many victims of abuse, I chose to take the blame for it all. A man does not have an excuse to rape an irresponsible teenager, *never, EVER.* I had to forgive that reckless teenager once and for all, finally have sympathy for what she endured, and give her peace by understanding it wasn't her fault.

Scientists tell us that every single cell in our body,

other than those in our cerebral cortex, is replaced within a seven-year cycle. With that in mind, understand that after seven years, our body that suffered whatever atrocity we endured and *survived* is now completely restored and made new. The only way to continue contaminating ourselves is to continue *thinking* about what happened from a place of pain, bitterness, and unforgiveness.

Let it go, sweet sister, for once and for all.

When we forgive, we let happiness, peace, and joy sit in the driver's seat of our lives.

.

CHAPTER TWELVE

THE ICING

Great news! There's an even more powerful tool at your disposal, and it can instantly neutralize every landmine in your minefield and truly help you avoid replanting them. Let me tell you how I discovered the tool and why I want to share it with you.

What I've shared so far helped me go from a very dysfunctional place in my early 20s to become a highly successful, independently wealthy, happy person by the time I hit my early 30s. If I had written this book then, the previous chapter would have been my stopping point. The virtual cake I baked for you, along with the tools I've made available at my website (www. truth.coach), would be enough to satisfy your needs. Thankfully, I have since found out about the icing that's available to top the cake and would love to share that with you as well.

I thought I had it all figured out; I was large and in charge; I was the master of my own universe and in total control. I always believed in God and His Son and went to church most Sundays, but I didn't see the need to talk to Him much because I had this whole "life" thing working great. As I said before, I was "in religion, not relationship." I had no idea of the level of peace, joy, and love that existed beyond an intellectual and detached understanding of God.

Like many people, I didn't truly find Him until my life fell apart, until I sought Him because I had no answers for the problems facing me. He was always right there waiting, but I was too busy chasing after money and other things society told me were important. I thought (like many people) if I could make enough money, I would be able to parlay that into happiness.

Many people, as I was doing, use money to reward themselves for being miserable all week. We justify a job or relationship that robs us of our joy because we can afford to spend the weekend doing the thing that truly brings us happiness. You see it everywhere—people working 60 hours a week so they can go boating, partying, or even just collapse in front of the TV.

This changed for me. For the last ten-plus years, in every aspect of my life—mental, emotional, financial, social, spiritual, and physical—God has been the greatest defuser of all the landmines I planted. I know I was good, but, **WOW**, is He greater!

What is your true relationship with God and His Son?

Have you been too busy to figure it out, just like I was for almost forty years?

Did some human pastor or priest do or say something wrong to you, and ever since you've been blaming God?

Perhaps you don't understand the Bible and it scares and confuses you?

Are you living life on your own terms, and you don't want a bunch of rules shoved down your throat?

Perhaps you can't stand judgmental Christians? Join the club.

At one point in my life, I fit into every single category listed above. In fact, I *still* can't tolerate judgmental Christians.

Who's better to guide us and help us navigate this fallen, crazy world than the One who has known the *true* us since before the Earth was even created? He knows every desire of our heart, He knows the purpose for our life, He knows how to eventually work every bad situation for our good. He even knows how many hairs are on our head.

Who in this world knows us this well? He even knows us better than we know ourselves.

So why in the world wouldn't we go to Him for help? If you're like me, it's because we were told to do things for ourselves, from the earliest time we can remember. And, quite frankly, we've learned to think, "Why do I want to bother God with my petty little problems? He has enough to worry about."

This way of thinking is just what the enemy wants. He doesn't want God smack dab in the middle of our lives giving us counsel. This way of thinking is a lie from Satan himself.

Here's the truth: God wants to be involved in everything going on in our lives, our family, our jobs, our friends, our significant others and spouses, our finances, our physical health, *everything!*

When was the last time you prayed about your family's friendships? Your kids' future spouses? Your next career move? Your financial strength used to bless others?

There is so much power in prayer, in asking for Gods' help and wisdom.

God gave us free will, and it's both a blessing and a curse. We humans tend to want to do everything our own way without consulting God on any of it; then when things don't go well, we demand for God to show up and fix it for us.

Think of God as our Daddy, as a parental figure. If you're a parent, this metaphor will be easy to understand:

You go out to your garage and you see your 14-year-old dismantling your family car. You drag him inside and tell him not to do it but, day after day, you keep catching him in the garage trying to take that car apart. You start implementing small disciplinary actions; they don't work. You start stepping up the discipline, and it still doesn't work. You finally have to resort to really harsh punishment and that finally deters him for the time being.

Fast-forward a few years; he now has his own car that you so generously bought for him, and guess what? The first Saturday he owns it, you go out to the garage to find him dismantling his brand-new car. Well, he's old enough now and you had told him it was a gift with no strings attached. (Who does that? A great and loving God does that all the time with our gift of life.)

As a parent, at some point we have to turn our kids over to themselves if they won't seek or accept our counsel

All you can do is offer your help and expertise as a master mechanic. You say, "Hey son, need any help?"

He replies "Nope, got this, mom, thanks." You're worried so you go back out to check on him an hour later. You really don't want to see him destroy what he's been given. It looks bad.

You ask again, almost pleading, "Sure you don't want some help? I would love to teach you what I know about cars, and this is the perfect opportunity."

Again, he replies, "Nope, got this, mom, thanks."

The end of the weekend approaches and you go back out to check on him. The car is in a thousand pieces and he's sitting in the middle of the chaos he made, sobbing.

He looks up at you, and he has one of two reactions. Either he blames you and starts screaming things like "How could you let me do this? Why didn't you stop me? What kind of parent lets their kid do something like this?" Or, he looks up at you with regret and remorse for what he has done, and he asks for your help.

As a parent, at some point we have to turn our kids over to themselves if they won't seek or accept our counsel.

How many times have *we* made a mess of things because *we* didn't seek God's counsel in the first place? Then we feel guilty, and we say things to ourselves like, "I made this mess, I need to fix it," when God is right there waiting, desperately wanting to step in to help, but we never ask.

Finally, when things are a total disaster, we either blame God or we finally seek Him. And just like we do when our kids look up at us in total helplessness and we dive in to help them get things back on track, so does our ever-loving, ever-merciful, ever-wise Father step in to help *us*.

Most (if not all) of us have made really important prayers that God never answered. A big one for me was when I was standing over a loved one who was about to die way too soon. I asked God, I pleaded, I flat-out begged. I'm sure my life is completely different because I lost my dad when I was only 19, and I have countless moments of sadness for what he missed in my life.

The big things he missed stand out: walking me down the aisle and giving me away; the father/daughter dance at my wedding reception; getting to know his beautiful grandchildren; and, especially, the laughs we would have shared. To this day, no one makes me laugh like my dad always did.

As painful as losing him was, thankfully I do know that my dad's death wasn't God's "fault."

None of us know when our time is up or how it all fits together in the big picture. Our ways are not God's ways, and our way of thinking is certainly not God's way of thinking. Someday, I'll get to sit down with Him and see how all of it was woven together to produce the tapestry of my life. Meanwhile, when I look back, I see how God used every hurt that I endured to help me grow into someone that I am very happy to be.

If this isn't the God you know, you don't have all the facts. I'm not saying *I* do, but I'm sharing with you what God has done and what he revealed in my life in the hope that you choose to seek the same amazing relationship with Him. He is love, He is joy, He is peace, and He wants to pour blessings into your life. He is the God of recompense, redemption, and restoration, and he's *not* the God of force.

One of my only regrets in life is that I didn't know how to lead my dad to God. My dad's alcoholism tormented him and tortured our family. When I was in my mid-teens, his health was hanging by a thread. His doctor told him that he couldn't even have one more sip of alcohol or he would die. My dad somehow stopped drinking, and after three years of sobriety, I thought he had finally defeated his demons.

I will never forget the night we were all out to dinner toasting my brothers' wedding. My dad was sitting next to me, and when everyone raised a glass, he grabbed mine. I looked at him with a combination of horror and anger, wanting to smack the glass out of his hand, and I knew in the pit of my stomach that I had just witnessed the beginning of the end.

> *He is love, He is joy, He is peace, and He wants to pour blessings into your life.*

The family spent another excruciatingly painful 12-18 months watching my dad drink himself to death before he breathed his last breath just as the doctor had warned. I pray that Jesus miraculously revealed Himself and my dad accepted Him as Truth and Savior in his final hours, but I won't know on this side of life.

I wish I had known how to tell my dad how much his Father loved him, the *whole* him, the *flawed* him, and that He longed to have a real relationship with him. God can only act in our lives if we invite Him in.

Unfortunately, I didn't yet know how to share this with my dad. I say this now to you, my sister, with passion and a total commitment to help our Father establish the loving relationship with you that He desperately wants.

I will say this again: God can only act in our lives if we invite Him in. It would truly be my honor to lead you in a prayer that will do just that. If you are ready, read this next part *out loud*. It's crucial that you say the words, so say them proudly:

Dear Lord,

I acknowledge that you, Jesus, are the Son of God. I believe that you died on the cross, that your blood was shed for my sins and that you arose from the grave and conquered death. I understand that I was born a sinner and that I have sinned by disobeying your commandments.

I ask you to forgive me for these sins. Please change my heart to be like yours, loving and full of forgiveness. Fill me with your Holy Spirit to help me obey your teachings as recorded in the Bible. Bring me people who can help me on my new path.

Be my Savior. Be my Lord. Thank you for saving me from death and giving me new life.

Amen.

Welcome to the family, and welcome to a whole new you! I would love to connect with you.

I warmly and sincerely invite you to join those of us committed to living a landmine-free life. I believe that if we're not moving forward through personal growth, then we are moving backwards; there is no "neutral."

Visit my website (www.truth.coach) for additional tools and support. As I shared with you earlier, I would *love* to work with you in person at one of my workshops.

Be blessed, my sister!

A Gift of Additional Tools

I would like to leave you with a few more tools and concepts to encourage and strengthen you.

The Truth in the Bible

I also want to bless you with scriptural truths for each of the landmines we covered. Scriptures always help you reinforce the truth: *God knows the struggles we go through, and the Bible is His love letter* to us and *for us*.

All verses are from The English Standard Version of the Bible (ESV) unless identified otherwise. I love this translation of God's word and keep a copy as my personal Bible, because the scripture is written in language that feels comfortable to read and say out loud. At the same time, the language has just enough majesty that every verse reminds me it comes straight from God.

Insecurity

Is it not from the mouth of the Most High that good and bad come? *Lamentations 3:38*

And we know that for those who love God all things work together for good, for those who are called according to his purpose. *Romans 8:28*

For the king trusts in the LORD, and through the steadfast love of the Most High he shall not be moved. *Psalm 21:7*

Humble yourselves, therefore, under the mighty hand of God so that at the proper time he may exalt you, casting all your anxieties on him, because he cares for you. *1 Peter 5:6-7*

Victim Mentality

Who shall separate us from the love of Christ? Shall tribulation, or distress, or persecution, or famine, or nakedness, or danger, or sword? No, in all these things we are more than conquerors through him who loved us. *Romans 8:35,37*

I can do all things through him who strengthens me. *Philippians 4:13*

Gossiping

Do not be deceived: "Bad company ruins good morals." *1 Corinthians 15:33*

Owe no one anything, except to love each other,

for the one who loves another has fulfilled the law. For the commandments, "You shall not commit adultery, You shall not murder, You shall not steal, You shall not covet," and any other commandment, are summed up in this word: "You shall love your neighbor as yourself." Love does no wrong to a neighbor; therefore love is the fulfilling of the law. *Romans 13:8-10*

Therefore, let us not pass judgment on one another any longer, but rather decide never to put a stumbling block or hindrance in the way of a brother. *Romans 14:13*

Let each of us please his neighbor for his good, to build him up. *Romans 15:2*

Backstabbing

Everyone utters lies to his neighbor; with flattering lips and a double heart they speak. *Psalm 12:2*

A gossip goes around telling secrets, but those who are trustworthy can keep a confidence. *Proverbs 11:13, New Living Translation (NLT)*

One who is righteous is a guide to his neighbor, but the way of the wicked leads them astray. *Proverbs 12:26*

Offendable

Therefore, you have no excuse, O man, every one of you who judges. For in passing judgment on another you condemn yourself, because you, the judge, practice the very same things. *Romans 2:1*

It is dangerous to be concerned with what others think of you, but if you trust the LORD, you are safe. *Proverbs 29:25, Good News Translation (GNT)*

Good sense makes one slow to anger, and it is his glory to overlook an offense. *Proverbs 19:11*

Why do you see the speck that is in your brother's eye, but do not notice the log that is in your own eye? Or how can you say to your brother, 'Let me take the speck out of your eye,' when there is the log in your own eye? You hypocrite, first take the log out of your own eye, and then you will see clearly to take the speck out of your brother's eye. *Matthew 7:3-5*

Mommy Guilt

Train up a child in the way he should go; even when he is old he will not depart from it. *Proverbs 22:6*

Behold, children are a heritage from the LORD, the fruit of the womb a reward. *Psalm 127:3*

She is clothed with strength and dignity, and she laughs without fear of the future. When she speaks, her words are wise, and she gives instructions with kindness. *Proverbs 31:25-26 (NLT)*

Do not be anxious about anything, but in everything by prayer and supplication with thanksgiving let your requests be made known to God. And the peace of God, which surpasses all understanding, will guard your hearts and your minds in Christ Jesus. *Philippians 4:6-7*

Comparison

Not that we dare to classify or compare ourselves with some of those who are commending themselves. But when they measure themselves by one another and compare themselves with one another, they are without understanding. *2 Corinthians 10:12*

Each of you must examine your own actions. Then you can be proud of your own accomplishments without comparing yourself to others. Assume your own responsibility. *Galatians 6:4-5, GOD'S WORD Translation (GW)*

For as in one body we have many members, and the members do not all have the same function, so we, though many, are one body in Christ, and individually members one of another. Having gifts that differ according to the grace given to us, let us use them: if prophecy, in proportion to our faith; *Romans 12:4-6*

Doubt

I can do all things through Christ who strengthens me. *Philippians 4:13, Jubilee Bible 2000 (JUB)*

Do not be anxious about anything, but in every situation, by prayer and petition, with thanksgiving, present your requests to God. *Philippians 4:6, New International Version (NIV)*

If any of you lacks wisdom, let him ask God, who gives generously to all without reproach, and it will be given him. But let him ask in faith, with no doubting, for the one who doubts is like a wave of the sea that is driven and tossed by the wind. For that person must not suppose that he will receive anything from the Lord; he is a double-minded man, unstable in all his ways. *James 1:5-8*

What then shall we say to these things? If God is for us, who can be against us? *Romans 8:31*

Therefore I tell you, do not be anxious about your life, what you will eat or what you will drink, nor about your body, what you will put on. Is not life more than food, and the body more than clothing? Look at the birds of the air: they neither sow nor reap nor gather into barns, and yet your heavenly Father feeds them. Are you not of more value than they? And which of you by being anxious can add a single hour to his span of life? And why are you anxious about clothing? Consider the lilies of the field, how they grow: they neither toil nor spin, yet I tell you, even Solomon in all his glory was not arrayed like one of these. But if God so clothes the grass of the field, which today is alive and tomorrow is thrown into the oven, will he not much more clothe you, O you of little faith? Therefore do not be anxious, saying, 'What shall we eat?' or 'What shall we drink?' or 'What shall we wear?' For the Gentiles seek after all these things, and your heavenly Father knows that you need them all. But seek first the kingdom of God and his righteousness, and all these things will be added to you.

Therefore do not be anxious about tomorrow, for tomorrow will be anxious for itself. Sufficient for the day is its own trouble. *Matthew 6:25-34*

But he must ask in faith without any doubting, for the one who doubts is like the surf of the sea, driven and tossed by the wind. For that man ought not to expect that he will receive anything from the Lord, *being* a double-minded man, unstable in all his ways. *James 1:8. New American Standard Bible (NASB)*

Overemotional

Peace I leave with you; my peace I give to you. Not as the world gives do I give to you. Let not your hearts be troubled, neither let them be afraid. *John 14:27*

Like a city whose walls are broken through is a person who lacks self-control. *Proverbs 25:28 (NIV)*

You keep him in perfect peace whose mind is stayed on you, because he trusts in you. Trust in the LORD forever, for the LORD GOD is an everlasting rock. *Isaiah 26:3-4*

Negative Self-Talk

Finally, brethren, whatever is true, whatever is honorable, whatever is right, whatever is pure, whatever is lovely, whatever is of good repute, if there is any excellence and if anything worthy of praise, dwell on these things. *Philippians 4:8. (NASB)*

When my anxious thoughts multiply within me,

your consolations delight my soul. *Psalm 94:19 (NASB)*

...casting all your anxiety on him because he cares for you. *1 Peter 5:7*

No, in all these things we are more than conquerors through him who loved us. For I am sure that neither death nor life, nor angels nor rulers, nor things present nor things to come, nor powers, nor height nor depth, nor anything else in all creation, will be able to separate us from the love of God in Christ Jesus our Lord. *Romans 8:37-39*

Bitterness and Unforgiveness

See to it that no one fails to obtain the grace of God; that no "root of bitterness" springs up and causes trouble, and by it many become defiled. *Hebrews 12:15*

May the God of hope fill you with all joy and peace in believing, so that by the power of the Holy Spirit you may abound in hope. *Romans 15:13*

But the fruit of the Spirit is love, joy, peace, patience, kindness, goodness, faithfulness...*Galatians 5:22*

Let all bitterness and wrath and anger and clamor and slander be put away from you, along with all malice. Be kind to one another, tenderhearted, forgiving one another, as God in Christ forgave you. *Ephesians 4:31-32*

And when you stand praying, if you hold anything against anyone, forgive them, so that your Father in heaven may forgive you your sins. *Mark 11:25 (NIV)*

For if you forgive others their trespasses, your heavenly Father will also forgive you, but if you do not forgive others their trespasses, neither will your Father forgive your trespasses. *Matthew 6:14-15*

The Icing

The LORD is my shepherd; I shall not want. He makes me lie down in green pastures. He leads me beside still waters. He restores my soul. He leads me in paths of righteousness for his name's sake. Even though I walk through the valley of the shadow of death, I will fear no evil, for you are with me; your rod and your staff, they comfort me. You prepare a table before me in the presence of my enemies; you anoint my head with oil; my cup overflows. Surely goodness and mercy shall follow me all the days of my life, and I shall dwell in the house of the LORD forever. *Psalm 23*

Other Biblical Tools

You can buy Bibles, bible studies in book or video form, Christian music, and a wealth of supplemental supplies in regular bookstores, Christian stores, and online. My

favorite website is Lifeway.com; I stock up on all kinds of reading and listening material there.

You don't absolutely need to have a printed version of the Bible these days. If you use your tablet or phone for reading or inspiration, you'll be comfortable using an app.

Though I will always cherish and read my printed version of the Bible, I also use the Life Church Bible app on a daily basis; its icon shown here. It is so reassuring to have the Bible with me, wherever I go.

ABOUT GAIL MCWILLIAMS

I asked Gail's loving and devoted husband Tony to write about her so you could garner a better understanding of the remarkable, brave woman who inspired me to write this book for all of you.

Kelly Accetta has accepted the challenge to write this book and has, by evidence of these very pages, successfully risen to the occasion. Typical to the kind of challenges Gail McWilliams dispensed to her audiences—and to her new-found friend in one Kelly Accetta—it is not surprising the kind of interchange Gail had with Kelly, and which is revealed in the introduction of this book.

Such an interchange is not unlike the one Gail had when she, too, was challenged by Zig Ziglar to write her own story. Gail had been invited to speak to a small group of people at the Ziglar Corporation and was given thirty minutes to deliver her presentation.

In twenty-nine minutes she was finished, and I assisted her in sitting down on the front row. As Kelly has already pointed out, Gail was visually impaired and is why my assistance was needed to guide her to her chair. On only rare occasions did she ever go over the amount of time allotted her, in spite of the fact she could not see to read a clock.

When Zig Ziglar, the famous motivational speaker, took his place at the front of the room—upon Gail's bringing her speech to a conclusion—he stood there and made no sound whatsoever. I had enjoyed Gail's company long enough to know silence is unsettling to her. When you cannot see, the sounds and words of others are needed to help you be aware of what is developing in the room, otherwise the absence of such sound contributes to not knowing what *is* developing and you can become a bit unnerved. Because I knew this was the case, I leaned toward Gail's ear and updated her via a whisper, "Mr. Ziglar is weeping."

Mr. Ziglar's silence because of his weeping, gave him a few extra moments to calm himself so he could speak. Once he began his communication, the first thing out of his mouth was a passionate plea, "Gail, you must write your story for the masses." This was truly a compliment and a kindness, but Gail did not take it seriously. She initially marked it up as perhaps the way he compliments all the guest speakers who come to his corporation. But upon further interchange, after the meeting was dismissed, it became important to know that Mr. Ziglar was quite serious.

During the next year, and with the help of talking software, Gail wrote and completed her own manuscript. Upon delivering *Seeing Beyond: Choosing to Look Past the Horizon* to Mr. Ziglar, he welcomed the request to add his foreword to the book and give the published endeavor its launch.

What was interesting about Gail McWilliams is she took the opportunities afforded her to pass on freely to others what she too had been given. Such was the case when she interchanged with Kelly. With nothing more than the words which Kelly spoke it was not hard for Gail to come to the conclusions she did, namely, that Kelly had a book in her and its title was obvious.

Gail had an uncanny ability to delve into the lives of new friends and find golden nuggets that they themselves barely realized were present. She could ask a series of short and poignant questions that made a demand on new acquaintances to dig deep. These people walked away from an encounter with Gail only to realize, like Kelly, that there is in them deposits and corresponding stories that need telling.

Another incident drives this point home. We had entered a small elevator and present with us was a man in a wheelchair. Because Gail could not know about the wheelchair from observation, I simply provided that information for her. It would have been awkward if she had said nothing when I announced, "Gail, there's a man in the elevator with us who is sitting in a wheelchair." But because I knew she was inclined to come alive in conversation, once she had that information in hand, I felt no qualms in providing such data. I learned this through the years and is why Gail was a quality individual who loved an encounter with others.

I stood there during those few short moments to observe some details Gail could not possibly have noticed. The man had a short haircut and protruding from his scalp and through his short hair were several unsightly scars, that anyone could observe. With nothing more than the fact that his skull was scattered with such scars I suppose I could have taken an educated guess to know why he was in the wheelchair. A horrendous accident of some kind perhaps. But, of course, Gail's ability to get right to the point superseded my reluctance to make the inquiry myself. She asked, "How did you get in the wheelchair?" So much for niceties when getting to the point might work even better.

In less than a minute the man told a quick,

gruesome story about abuse by a baby sitter when he was a kid. What was interesting is Gail took this moment to delve into his life's story, and the encouragement that came from her, as it always did, was so apropos, including a heartfelt thank you from Gail for his telling the story.

What also developed during those short precious moments in an elevator ride from floor two to floor one is when the friends that had accompanied their wheelchair-bound friend announced, "We didn't know that." We took notice of this last comment more than anything. His friends didn't even know his story. Gail used this incident to encourage others that all people have stories to tell, and they need the opportunity to tell that story. It adds a sense of worth to their person and a sense of purpose to their struggles.

Gail found a way to encourage people in spite of her own struggles, which were many, and at the end of her life those struggles were intense. She slipped into eternity on the morning of Christmas Eve, 2016. She leaves behind a legacy of people encouraged to do what is in their heart.

Kelly was right. Gail was a blind person who sees better than most. Gail told us that she practiced seeing and she encouraged us to look beyond the horizon where the sky's the limit. This would certainly mean giving serious attention to the insights about defusing landmines that Kelly points out in this book.

I agree with Kelly. You are simply too amazing to do otherwise.

For more information about this amazing woman, Gail McWilliams, and her work, please visit her website, www. GailMcWilliams.com.

I hope this book in its entirety has blessed you.

ACKNOWLEDGMENTS

First and foremost, I thank God. He truly orchestrated this book from concept to conclusion, and He will be fully in charge of taking it to the masses of women who need to know His deep, unconditional, head-over-heels love. I am honored to be the vessel He has chosen to deliver this book to you.

My family has been *amazingly* supportive, and I give them all special thanks. It's never easy to allow our private life and struggles to go under public scrutiny. Thanks to my mom, who has been the biggest cheerleader in my life, and to my grandfather, Art, who told me over and over again that I could be *anything* I wanted to be in life. Thanks to my brothers: Brian, who has always been and will always be my rock, and Kevin, who taught me so many valuable lessons. Thanks to my loving Aunt Vicki and her amazingly talented husband, Michael, who spent so many hours helping this book be the best it could be. Thank you, Alex and Nicole, for allowing me to tell all my stories about you to the world. Thank you, Marc, for being an incredible father to our girls and a mentor/business partner/husband to me for 26 years. And thanks to the rest of my family: Dave, Erin, Lauren, J.P., Iraida, Aunt Shirley, Uncle Jim, Nana, Grammy, Grand Tommy, and my dad, for just flat out loving me and teaching me so much!

A handful of friends have walked with me through some of my darkest times, and I want to thank you all for your love. My pastors, Mike and Kathy Hayes, you have no idea how much your love and support has strengthened me. Nancy Lieberman, I will cherish your friendship for the rest of my days. You have been and will always be there for me, and I will be there for you! Fenton Fulgham, you are truly my spiritual brother, and I am so grateful for your love, support and friendship. Susan Mittan, my spiritual advisor and sister, God truly put you in my life at the appointed time. I trusted you with things I thought I could never share with anyone; you gave me the strength and the biblical insight to know that I must do so. Kimberly Bliquez, thank you for your spiritual counsel and love. And thank you, Mari Rubio, Frances Gonzalez, and Anthany Arosarena for all of the tears, laughter, and wine we shared.

I would also like to thank my many amazing girlfriends from around the world who have shared their stories, hearts, and love with me. You all are threads that have been woven into the tapestry of my life, and I am so grateful to God for each and every one of you! Amie Dockery, Kim Atkinson, Cindy Bolf, Courtney Tyler, Crystal Wimbrey, Susan Nugent, Valerie Acosta, Efrosyni Adamides, Shelly Alford, Maria Anessi, Ivette Arecena, Amy Avila, Shannon Balster, Anel Bangs, Lynn Blake, Marla Blake, Nicki Bolz, Kathy Brown, Brandi Crosby, Helen Bundschu, Melanie Capps, Wendy Castillo, Marilyn Chapman, Alice Chou, Tarah Davis, Donza Doss, Shirley Dwek, Misty DeMelo, Kristin Finley, Margie Frank, Franchesca German, April Gilliland, Jill Hellwig, Christina Helms, Kathy Hill, Stephanie Holmes, Stacy Horowitz, Kat Iheke, Nancy Kevorkian, Jully Law, Melanie Levitz, Amber Lee, Millie Leung, Kimberly Martin, Cindy Malawey, Rita Mayberry, Diane McKnight, Me Ra Koh, Rhonda Morris, Lara Mouritzen, Kerrie Oles, Tenia Padilla, Melinda Perez, Trudy Powell, Sari Poremba, Jodi Prior, Shawn Reed, Megan Santos, Kari and Lisha Schneider, Susan Shrag, Kara Siffermann, Tracy Stammen, Shuvawn Sweet, Dee Telting, SuSu Thomas, Sara Thompson, Amanda Trippi, Yvette Ulloa, Kristi Walker, Peggy White, Tiffany Williams, Melina Wright, Sandra Yancey, and all my Cuba girls! There are so many more of you; please forgive me if you weren't named specifically in the list above—we could have listed five more pages of your names! I am equally blessed by *all* of you as well. Also, a huge shout-out to my all my guy friends; your perspective was invaluable!

And lastly, I would like to thank my publisher, Michael Vezo at Westcom Press. The incredible team that you introduced me to is such a blessing: Chris Flynn for my cover art, and the talented and extremely patient editor, J. McCrary.

(Raymond, the next few years are about to get crazy, so I thank you in advance for your love, support and patience.)

56416649R00080

Made in the USA
Columbia, SC
24 April 2019